FIFTY YEARS DOWN THE DRAIN

*   *   *

The Collected Portilla Poems of Robert Rahula

1969-2019

ALSO BY ROBERT RAHULA

NOVELS:
Messieurs
Panamaniac
Island of Misfits
Day Another Paradise In
One Last Fling
Bathhouse Stories
Conversation in a Belgian Bar
All the Yage in Reno
Exigent Circumstances
Uninvited Guest
A Modest Summation of Things

SHORT STORIES:
Horror Stories for Children

POETRY:
Trigger Points
Dentro Del Corazón Bloqueada
Camino
Migration
I Sing the Body Politic
Wonderland
From Whose Bourn
Poemas Españoles
Expat Poems

ANTHOLOGIES:
Half Life
The Essential Dan Landes

FIFTY YEARS DOWN THE DRAIN
THE COLLECTED PORTILLA POEMS
OF ROBERT RAHULA
1969-2019

© 2020 by Robert Rahula

All rights reserved. This book or any portion thereof may not be reproduced or used in any manner whatsoever without the express written permission of the author except for the use of brief quotations in a book review.

www.robertrahula.com

This is a work of fiction. Characters, organizations, businesses, products, locales, and events portrayed in this book either are products of the author's imagination or are used fictitiously.

Acknowledgements:
This collection consists of poems drawn from the following books:
Trigger Points © 2013
Dentro Del Corazón Bloqueada © 2013
Camino © 2014
Migration © 2014
I Sing the Body Politic © 2015
Wonderland © 2016
From Whose Bourne © 2017

Special thanks to Liz Shine and Chris House at Red Dress Press for all their help, editing and design.

ISBN 978-1-7329708-5-4

Alma-gator Press
Barcelona • Madrid • La Chorrera

*"Life is like rowing a boat to the middle of a lake...
and drowning.
There's nothing negative about it,
except for, you know, the drowning part."*

-Robert Rahula

TABLE OF CONTENTS

Introduction by Joseph Wambatten

HOW TO REMOVE A TATTOO	19
WHEN I KNEW CHARLES	20
PANDORA	24
MY PLEASURE	25
YOU WERE SO BEAUTIFUL	26
MILES TO GO	28
WAKE ME WHEN IT'S OVER	29
AN EVENING WITH TRIGGER	30
THE SIMPLE PLEASURES	32
SPEECHLESS	34
OLDER NOW	37
THAT FIRST NIGHT WITH TRIGGER	38
MR. LINK	39
IT WAS LIKE THIS, HE SAID	40
AZTEC TWO-STEP	41
LEARNING CURVE	40
THE DOLLHOUSE	43
LINES	49
NOT MUCH TO SAY	50
DOLLARS TO DOUGHNUTS	51
SHE HAS	52
TIME	53
COMMUNION	55
THE HARDWAYS	56
REVISIONIST	57
THE IMPACT OF THE OPPOSITE	58
THE DAY OF REST	60

BUDDHA IS TURNING IN HIS GRAVE.................61
THE OUTSIDER..................................62
VOYEUR..68
CURIOUS.......................................69
REPUBLICANS...................................71
BREAKING EVEN.................................73
THE MATERIALIZATION AND VAPORIZATION OF THOUGHT ITSELF.................................74
WHAT HAPPENS TO THESE WOMEN?..................75
LIFE..81
MEET AND GREET................................82
IAGO..84
SOMEONE FOR EVERYONE..........................85
SOBRIETY......................................86
SOME OF THE TIME..............................87
THANK YOU MICHAEL MALYSZKO....................90
WHAT LOVE IS..................................93
COSTUME PARTY.................................96
ON THE WAIT..................................100
BELOW THE SURFACE............................102
I SUPPOSE NORMAL PEOPLE MAKE NORMAL WEEKEND PLANS 104
WHEN WE WERE LOVERS..........................105
GROOMING BEHAVIOR............................107
THE CALIBER OF A PERSON......................108
KARMA..109
WHAT A PIECE OF WORK.........................111
EMBLEMS......................................112
INSIDE THE LOCKED HEART......................113
THIS IS HOW MY EVENINGS GO...................114

SPENDING TIME WITH MARY	118
WOMEN	119
ESCARGOT	121
ON KISSING	123
GYPSY	124
LIQUIDITY	128
SONOFABITCH	129
ODE TO ANNYA	130
TO YOU, HERBERT	134
HEAVEN'S CALL CENTER	136
DUCK BLIND	138
WHY I WRITE	139
THE WAY OF SAINT JAMES	141
LATE SEPTEMBER	143
THE LONG ROAD	144
THE JUDGE	145
EVERYNIGHT	146
DURABLE POWER OF ATTORNEY	147
SOMETHING	148
CLEANING UP	149
LAMENTATIONS	150
THE INVISIBLE MAN	153
PEOPLE I KNOW	154
WHEN ERNESTO GOT OUT OF PRISON	156
STREET LIFE	158
SALES CONFERENCE	159
DON'T LOOK NOW	160
IT CHANGES THROUGHOUT THE DAY	161
TRAIN WRECKS	162
RALPH WHITEWAY DIDN'T LIKE HIS NAME	163

MEMORIES ARE MADE OF THIS	164
WHAT WOMEN WANT	165
WHEN YOU GONNA WAKE UP?	166
STAND-OFF	168
MOON	169
DINNER	170
GIVE UP	171
THE BATHHOUSE	172
IN THE REALM OF INFINITE POSSIBILITIES	174
WHAT GOD WILL NOT FORGIVE	175
HOW ABOUT YOU?	176
FACEBOOK	178
TIM	179
CATALINA IS A BURNING TATTOO	180
MISS AMANDA	181
FARMERS MARKET	183
GOD'S WILL	184
WE LIVE OUR LIVES AS METAPHORS	186
ALI-CAT	189
NOTHING IS FREE	190
BANKING PROBLEMS	192
HARSH	194
AGUIRRE AND YOU AND ME	197
OVERHEARD	199
I DIDN'T KNOW	200
WHO DO WE THINK WE ARE?	201
THE GAME OF LOVE	203
OCCUPATIONAL HAZARD	204
WAITING ROOMS	205
HUNGER	206

THE REGULATION OF PEE	207
STARING AT THE WALL	208
NEW ORLEANS	209
WHEN THE MUSE SAYS GOODBYE	210
ANT TOWN	212
WHAT SAPPHO SAID TO APHRODITE	214
THEY THOUGHT THEY WERE FREE	216
SAY WHAT YOU WANT	218
EVER NOTICE	220
ALI SAID TO ME ONE TIME IN BED	222
ATTENTION SPAN	223
CRAPS	224
THE THING ABOUT ALI	225
CONDENSATION	227
DE MINIMIS	228
THE BARREL	229
IT'S A COMMON STORY	230
THE SIMPLE LIFE	231
PACHINKO	232
POETRY IN ACTION	233
STUCK	234
IN SOME MOVIE I SAW YEARS AGO	236
LAYS	237
TEMPUS FUGIT	238
THE LIST	239
WHEEL OF FORTUNE	240
INVITATIONS	241
THE TROUBLE WITH STORIES	243
XEN	244
WHAT HAPPENED TO US?	246

UNDER MY SKIN	247
THE CIRCLE OF LIGHT	249
REAL LIFE	250
KILLING TIME	251
PERFECT BREASTS	252
THAT THIN WHITE LINE	253
LISTS	255
SEARCHING FOR ONESELF	256
RELATIONSHIPS	257
THE HILLS GO BY LIKE YEARS	262
I HOPE I MAKE IT	263
PHALLUS IN WONDERLAND	264
WINTER FORECAST	265
CRESTING THE HILL	267
NOBODY LIKES FISHBONES	268
MR. KURTZ, HE DEAD	269
HEAVEN	270
IN A RUT	271
SOUND CHECK	272
TEACHING HORSES TO TALK	274
ASK SOMEONE WHO KNOWS	276
NAKED CITY	278
ALL THERE IS	279
THE AMERICAN HANDJOB	280
ME AND MARLON BRANDO	281
THE BLIND LOVING THE BLIND	282
HOME	286
WHAT THE ANGEL TOLD THE LITTLE BOY	288
JUST SITTING HERE THINKING	289
DREAMING OF DINOSAURS	293

ONE BECOMES ENCHANTED	294
ALICE'S RESTAURANT	295
MY SECRET LIFE	296
PROGRESS	297
IT'S JUST SAD	298
BAMBI75	300
GENTLY	301
TAMMY	302
METAPHOR METAMORPHOOUS	305
MINE FIELD	306
KILL FEE	308
SOMEWHERE IMPORTANT	309
ON WRITING POETRY	310
SEE YOU IN DREAMLAND	331
CALLER ID	312
DIVERSIONS	313
GALA	314
OLD LOVE LETTERS	315
R.I.P.	316
GHOST	317
SO MUCH FOR THE SINGULARITY	319
GENESIS	321
THE HARDEST PART	322
FROM WHOSE BOURN	323
GOD'S PLAN	324
LIFE BREAKS EVERYONE	325
STREET LEGAL	326
SHRUNKEN HEADS	327
GHOSTS FROM THE FUTURE	328
THE PRICE OF PARADISE	332

I LEFT THE BAR	334
GEOLOGY 101	335
THINK ABOUT IT	337
WHISPERS	338
ANOTHER DAMN POEM ABOUT LOVE	339
WHAT MARK RUDD DREAMS	340
LONG (STARRY STARRY) NIGHT	344
METAPHYSICS	348
DIVORCE	349
THE FUTURE	352
LAW OF THE JUNGLE	353
BEFORE MATH	354
HISTORY LESSONS	355
THE THINGS ONE LEARNS	357
MISDIRECTION	359
BUT YOU CAN	361
NO OTHER CHOICE	362

Introduction by Joseph Wambatten

After the success of Robert Rahula's first anthology of English poems published in the United States, entitled *Expat Poems,* his publisher approached me about the possibility of editing a definitive collection of Robert's poems—an anthology that would span his entire career. Having been Robert's friend and editor for over forty years, I readily agreed.

However, I did not realize what a daunting task this would be.

With *Expat Poems,* Robert had personally selected sixty-three of what he considered to be his best poems about the expatriate experience—the experience of the outsider, the wanderer, yearning to reconnect to a home that no longer exists. Robert certainly spoke from experience in this regard, having been born in Spain, growing up in the United States, returning to Spain as a young man, and then emigrating to Panama. My role in that project was simply as editor: proofreading and arranging the poems that Robert had selected.

However, for this book, Robert insisted that I make the selection of poems to be included in this volume. I assumed that this would be an easy task until Robert brought me over fifteen hundred poems—a life's work that spanned fifty years as a writer. We first determined that this book should only include English poems. (An anthology of his best known Spanish poems is available in his book *Poemas Españoles.*) And we further decided not to include any poems that were included in *Expat Poems.*

That narrowed the task down to nine hundred poems. The process of reading and selecting which poems to include gave me a new appreciation for Robert's life as a poet and the poetic style called *Portilla* which he helped establish in Spain in the late seventies. *Portilla* literally means porthole in Spanish, a small window in a ship from which a sailor can stare from his tiny confined cabin out to the vastness of the sea. Similar to the Fado songs of Portugal or the Boleros of Cuba, Portilla is a style of poetry that expresses a deep longing for some future reunion or memory of some idyllic past against the present reality of loneliness and separateness. There is always the ever-present awareness of death in Portilla poems. But unlike Fados or Boleros, Portilla poetry fends death off with a dark humor and copes with separateness by celebrating sexuality. Whereas the Fados and Boleros arose from the emotions of sailors at sea or the lovers they left behind in the coastal cities, Portillas emerged in the city of Madrid, deep in the heartland of Spain, during La Movida Madrileña — that explosion of free expression that erupted after the death of Franco. Young men and women were finally free to release their anger at the dictatorship that had confined them for so long, and finally free to explore sexual themes and practices that had been forbidden to them.

Robert was there during that time, reading his poems at the poetry readings that sprang up in bars and coffee shops of Madrid, listening to the other poets of his generation, crafting his art, and developing his own unique style of Portilla poetry. His poems are not arms-length intellectualisms, but poetic transcriptions of real life, with all its free-flowing sexual energy, and all of life's ecstasy, eventual deception, and pointless decay. He makes no apologies for his bisexual polyamorous appetite, nor for the solitude and separateness that flows through his life.

It was Robert who came up with the book's title. When I suggested that *Fifty Years Down the Drain* seemed a bit negative, considering the literary output of his life, he just laughed and said, "Well, that's all life is, you know. You climb into a little boat, row out to the middle of a lake, and drown. That's just life. Doesn't matter what you've accomplished. Everybody drowns. There's nothing negative about it...except for, you know, the drowning part." And so, we kept the title... and his quote.

Eventually, I selected 222 poems that best represent Robert's views on love, sex, bisexuality, excess, and death—poems that showed his dark humor and his will to survive despite the madness of it all.

I hope you find as much meaning in these poems as I do.

HOW TO REMOVE A TATTOO

Well you can cut it out, but usually there's a substantial loss of blood, not to mention muscle tissue, and the scar is kind of hard to explain to your friends... or you can have it lasered out, but that costs thousands of dollars and it often still leaves a ghost of the tattoo on your skin... or you can cover it with another tattoo if you can find a tattoo artist with enough skill...

But what about the invisible tattoos?... the ones that love... or hate... leave on your heart? How do you remove them? Do you take a knife to your own flesh? Make a quietus with bare bodkin? Do you rip out your heart screaming that you will never love again? Do you bleed every time you pass by the tattoo parlor or the clinic or the bar where you first met? How do you remove a tattoo? And what about the ones printed on you before you had a choice? Here's the tattoo of the victim kid... the renegade kid... the outsider... the abused... the forgotten left alone abandoned or worse the fingered kissed groped kid... How do you remove those tattoos? With a knife? With a laser? Or do you search the bars for another tattoo artist more skilled in violating your skin so he can cover that first bruise that first violation with his own ink? his own cum?... How do you remove an invisible tattoo? With knives? With cuts? With blood? With pain? With more ink? With more coke more meth more drink? With time?... Time... Time that softens and fades the harshest reds and blues? How do you remove a tattoo? I wish I knew.

WHEN I KNEW CHARLES

When I knew Charles
before he was murdered
he lived in this nice penthouse
and had these great parties
with lots of young women
and gay men
and great food.

I'm not sure where he got his money.
He claimed he had invented
a commercial oven for restaurants.
I did notice that he lived with his mother
in that nice penthouse
with the great parties.
But there was no question he had money.
It was well known that he had made
some shrewd investments in certain
Hollywood movies
and his name did appear in the credits
at the end with several other "producers."
Some of the young women and the gay men
at his parties were actors
and they thought Charles could get them
into movies
so they had sex with him.
He really had no ability to get them into movies
because he was just an investor
but he did not dissuade them of this illusion
and he had great ability to get them into bed.

His mother (who was way past sixty)
would attend the parties
that Charles threw in the penthouse

and she would occasionally pick out
some young man
to fuck her
which they did quite willingly.
Money is funny that way.
You'd see them whispering in the corner
and then she and the young man
would just slip away.
Charles' mother was discrete.

Charles, however, was not so discrete.
He liked the threesomes
and the foursomes and was quite
vocal about it.

When I met Charles
he was grooming some young ingénue.
She must have been about nineteen.
He showed me her picture
posing sexy in a bubble bath
and exclaimed "Isn't she beautiful?!"
Everything Charles said was an exclamation,
but she was not beautiful
at least not Hollywood beautiful.
She was just nineteen-year-old female flesh pretty,
but he had her on the hook
telling her how he was going to make her a star.
Of course she was fucking him.

When I knew Charles
before he was murdered
he took a fancy to me
(because at that time I was young)
and I didn't mind
because the stories of his threesomes

were well known
and I was interested in that,
being, as I say, young,
so when he showed me the photograph of his ingénue
I made sufficient subtle comment to let him know
that I would be open to the three of us
getting together.

A few nights later he called me
and I went over
and she was there
and, as I say, pretty.
She seemed distracted
maybe bored
but Charles didn't waste much time
and before too long
the three of us were fucking.
She put me in her front hole
while Charles fucked her rear.
I enjoyed it.
She didn't really say much
And afterwards she fell asleep.
I never saw her again.

A week later Charles called me
and I went over.
This time he had two other men there,
handsome lads.
There was no conversation.
We all just headed off to his bed
with its mirrored walls and mirrored ceiling.
I enjoyed that too.
Afterwards he made dinner for us all
in his marvelous kitchen,
cooked hamburgers in that special oven
he had invented.

I ran into Charles about six months later
at some Christmas party
and I asked him what became of his ingénue.
"Oh her!" he exclaimed, "well, she never could act that well."
which I suppose, in a sense, was true.

It was a number of years after that
that Charles was murdered.
He had picked up some hustler,
a very handsome hustler, I'm told,
who moved in with Charles
and they fucked day and night
for several weeks
but at some point Charles grew tired of him
and told him he had to leave
and the young man took umbrage at this
and stabbed Charles
with one of Charles' own kitchen knives.
Stabbed him ten times.
The marvelous kitchen, I'm told, was covered with blood.
The hustler was arrested.
The newspaper articles simply referred
to the hustler as a "roommate."

Charles was fifty-six when he died.

When I knew Charles
before he was murdered
he lived in this nice penthouse
and had these great parties.

PANDORA

Everyone gets to take one secret
to the grave
whether it's something you did
or something you didn't do
or something that happened to you...
a crime
an accident
an affair
a betrayal
whatever.
There are some things other people just don't need to know,
that you don't need to say
ever
ever
ever.

In the house of you
there is a dark room
and in that dark room
there is a secret closet
behind a fake wall
and in that secret closet
there is a trap door
in which is hidden
a locked box
and in that locked box
there is a secret
that must never be revealed
to anyone
and most importantly
never to you.

MY PLEASURE

Rebecca was unhappily married
when I met her,
and a few weeks later
as such things happen,
her husband was out of town
and I took her to a dark bar
where we had a drink
and where I kissed her.
Afterwards we drove to my apartment.

The sex was the desperate kind that people have
when they are very very hungry,
a lot of grappling, hard kissing, deep kissing,
and other acts of an oral and carnal nature,
as if we were trying to devour each other.
Afterwards we lay there exhausted
and then she said,
"Thanks, I needed that."

All these years later, that one sentence
sticks in my mind.
It's the kind of thing you'd expect a man to say,
"Thanks, I needed that," as opposed to
"That was great," or
"You were magnificent."
But Rebecca was just being honest.
She needed that,
and I just happened to be
in the right place at the right time
and, as such things happen,
I needed it too.

YOU WERE SO BEAUTIFUL

I was in Florida at an educational conference.
It was 1976
before AIDS even had a name
and there was this young handsome pianist
who played at the conference,
a beautiful man
a gifted musician
and, to me, obviously gay.
And a fan of his told me
how tragic it was that he kept getting sick
in and out of hospitals
with pneumonia
and no one could figure out why.
And one night he played the piano
and sang for us
a haunting rendition of
"You Are So Beautiful."
I was very impressed by him
and his talent.
And later we shared a drink at the bar
and he came on to me, because,
as I said, he was gay
and I was much younger back then
and, as they say, unattached.

Well, I don't know why I declined his offer,
but I did.

It's interesting.
We have no idea how many bullets we dodge,
how many train wrecks we avoid,
how many appointments with death we miss.
Do the angels protect us?

Do they whisper in our ear?
I have no idea why I declined his offer,
but I did.

MILES TO GO

It appears my wine glass is empty,
and I have miles to go before I sleep.
So let us go then, you and I,
back to the kitchen to fill the glass high.
Just a second glass for the roses
or the hoses
or for you and I here among these noses.
For it yet remains to see
if immortality will unveil a
third glass for me.
But if I had to perish twice
I would pick a chardonnay on ice.
Yes, this is the way the world ends,
not with a bang, but with a merlot.

WAKE ME WHEN IT'S OVER

They call her Trigger
because she's high-spirited, they say.
Of course, trigger can also mean
hair-trigger
on the gun aimed at your heart.
Well, my my
I like her laugh
but my my
I've been down that road before...
Married twice... Jesus Christ,
let me take the road never traveled.
Look at those tattoos
my my
I'm a sucker for hair pulled back
my my
but haven't I seen those fangs before?
the hammer pulled back
a soft click in the darkness...
Luckily,
I am not her target.
I pull out my AARP card.
Luckily,
I am out of range.

AN EVENING WITH TRIGGER

She wants to have dinner out.
I tell her I have no money.
She tells me she can't get away until after seven.
I tell her I will have already eaten by then.
She says she will call me later.

I am asleep when she comes by. (No call.)
She says she is hungry. (I have already eaten.)
I offer my homemade soup,
but she wants to eat at her favorite Thai restaurant.
I tell her I will have tea.
She orders enough food for three.
I eat some.
It is good.
The bill comes. We split the meal. She'll take the leftovers home.

She complains that her stomach hurts.
Too many sit-ups with the personal trainer.
I don't care.

She wants to go to Walmart.
I go with.
She buys an exercise pad, glucosamine, vitamins, protein bars, muscle milk, etc.
We look at baby clothes.
She tells me that when she had her abortion, she coped by buying lots of baby clothes.

She asks me whether she will ever get married.
I tell her that I guarantee she will.
(Men are fools.)

We go to Walgreens
to buy more antioxidants.
She examines the vitamins.
I look at the toy handcuffs.

She drops me off at home.
She says she had a wonderful time.
Can she see me tomorrow?
I tell her I have to work.
She says she will call me.

THE SIMPLE PLEASURES

I know, I know,
you've heard it before.
The same old story
but I have to tell it again.
Trigger wanted to go watch the ocean tonight
so she came by and picked me up.

It is a nice beach, after all.
And I enjoy the waves and the setting sun.
It's a simple pleasure.
But she starts telling me
for the *millionth* time
how the ex-boyfriend called her
and *she is so done with him* and
why does he hurt her so?
and I listen quietly
and then point out for the millionth time
that he does it because she lets him do it,
and she could simply tell him "stop calling me"
but she doesn't ever say that.

The setting sun is brilliant
and warm on my face.
I like it.
I like the sound of the incoming waves.
We're sitting on rough rocks about ten feet above the waves.
I like the sound of them hitting on the rocks.
It's the simple pleasures.

She tells me that he's been texting her all day
sending pictures of antique stores he's been to.
"He never wanted to go antiquing with me," she says.
"Uh huh," I say, and listen to the waves.

I like a glass of wine with a meal.
I like simple cheeses.
I like the smell of summer.
I like the setting sun on the water.

"Do you think I'm losing weight?" she asks.
"Yes," I say.
"Why does he call me if he doesn't want me?"
"I don't know," I say, "do you want him?"
"No," she says.
"Then what does it matter why he calls you? Cut him loose," I say.
"I should," she says.
She won't.
This has been going on for ten months.
It's the simple pleasures that give life meaning,
like drowning in your own piss
and milking the drama
and talking only about yourself.
You know,
the simple pleasures.

SPEECHLESS

I don't know what to say sometimes when you call me.
I always love it when you call me,
but I never know where to begin.
You're there with your man,
I'm here with ghosts.
Yes, I'm still seeing Trigger.
Yes, I am in love with her,
in my kind of love.
No, she doesn't want me.
She just wants to be wanted.
She just wants to be adored.
It's so sad.
I would be the one to cure her, but I can't cure her.
I just can't. There's not enough love in this world to cure her.
I am so seduced by beauty.
I love beauty.
How ironic.
I, who am growing old,
yet only now appreciate beauty.

I don't know what to say sometimes when you call me.
I always love it when you call me,
but I don't know where to begin.
Shall I say I am Lazarus brought back from the dead by beauty?

Trigger asked me to help her dye her hair again.
That means helping her naked into the shower,
handing her chemicals, neutralizers, and towels.
I need a neutralizer for my heart
or my loins.
I just want a girlfriend who isn't crazy self-absorbed insane stupid deceptive etc.

Why is that so hard?
I'm not such a bad guy;
just over the hill, broken, left-over, jaded, tired, tired of
people, not much to offer here.
I give up.
I just give up.
I should just go back to being gay.
Bring on the uncomplicated boys.
They don't want to be adored—they just want
uncomplicated sex.
But the problem is, I really like women.
I like the way they smell. I like the way they feel.
I like the way they look.

I don't know what to say sometimes when you call me.
I always love it when you call me,
but I don't know where to begin.
I told her I wanted to be honest. I told her how I felt.
She told me that if things were different she would know
how she felt.
What does that mean?
I want to dig a hole and bury my heart.
I don't want to care about anyone anymore.

What is beauty?
Many Germans thought Hitler handsome.
Women wrote Ted Bundy offering to marry him.
Why are we so immediately seduced by beauty
even when beauty tells us nothing about the person?
I know there is no answer for this.
I only know that every woman that I have loved,
I have thought they were beautiful.
I confess my shallowness.
I love beauty.
I love beautiful women.

(I would love beautiful men if they smelled as good as beautiful women.)
I love sex.
I love the tender moments, the awkward moments, the ooooh moments.
Those moments are rare.
(More rare than they used to be.)

I don't know what to say sometimes when you call me.
I always love it when you call me,
but I don't know where to begin.
I do think that I, like Lazarus, am actually back from the dead.
I wander through these moments, these memories, like villages,
and I feel dead.
I was kissing Trigger and I could tell she was just letting me kiss her
and not kissing me back.
I don't need to be patronized.
I don't need to be played for the fool that I am.

I could tell you more but it would just be the same refrain like a blues record
that says, hey baby doncha do me wrong do da do da do da.
I came home today and hung up my jacket,
microwaved my dinner,
drank some wine.
You called. We talked,
and I wrote this.

OLDER NOW

One is always older
As time goes on.
Life gets colder.
There's a lady at work
Who's also older
Yet not older than me.
Between hope and shadow
Is always some possibility.

One more unbuttoning
One more fumbling
One more removing
Of blouses, bras, etc.
Is this too much to ask?

Older now
More cautious
More insecure
More testing of the waters
Before we dive in.
But dive in we must.
It is our destiny,
Our desire,
Our raison d'etre.

And the great philosophical questions about the meaning
Of life pale against
The more basic questions
Of good hygiene
And the hope of great mounds of pubic hair.

THAT FIRST NIGHT WITH TRIGGER

I was going to write a few lines about love
or rather,
my lack thereof.
But when I sat down,
I happened to think of you.

You know,
I did love you once.
I remember one particular night
on the porch
when love was new
and you told me
you liked my soft lips.

That was almost two years ago.
Seems like decades now.
I no longer know where you are,
although I know
with the internet
I could find you.
I choose not to.

I prefer to remember you
that night on the porch.
We each held a glass of wine
and kissed for the first time
and you said
"I knew your lips would be soft"
which made me happy
that you had wanted me before that kiss.

I'm glad we didn't stop with that first kiss.
And yet I'm glad I no longer know where you are.
Love is weird that way.

MR. LINK

When I was a manager
    at Circuit City
sometimes we would decide to fire someone
    for not making their sales goals
and we'd pick a certain date to do it
and the fellow would come in every day
    and do his job
        totally ignorant that his termination
        was coming up in a few days.
And on the morning of his final day
    he'd come in.
"Hello Bob," we'd say, "howya doing?"
and we'd let him work the day.
Then at five o'clock we'd call him in
    and give him the ax.

Death is like this.
It knows the date of our termination.
It waits.

And we wake up in the morning and we hear
"Hello, howya doing?"
"Fine," we say, and get out of bed.

IT WAS LIKE THIS, HE SAID

It was like this, he said, I was sitting at the bar minding my own business when this dude who I never seen before starts hassling this girl who was working there and that's not right you know so I told him to stop and he asked me who the fuck I thought I was so I popped him in the head to show him who the fuck I was and then the police showed up but I made it out the back door down the alley and got into my car and hauled ass out of there but then I look in the mirror and there's flashing lights and they pull me over for following too close... I mean dude that's a bullshit charge following too close and then they get me out of the car and I don't have my license on me and they run my name and there's this old warrant I swear I thought I had paid it but it's still in the system so they arrest me and when we get down to the jail they say they found meth in my pocket so they charge me with trying to smuggle drugs into the jail man that's a bullshit charge I was in cuffs how could I be smuggling and besides they were the ones taking me to jail and it wasn't meth and it wasn't my meth because I had gotten up that morning and my clothes were dirty so I just grabbed my roommate's jeans it must have been his meth and this arrest really fucks with my plans because I was going to leave this fucking county tomorrow . . . So man, can you get me out of jail?

AZTEC TWO-STEP

I figure I'm doing
the Aztec two-step.
You know the game:
the gods give you paradise
for a year,
make you the king,
for a year,
and everything is beautiful.
You're the golden boy,
everything you wanted is yours.
And then
when the year is up
they march you
up the stairs
of the altar
and rip out your heart.

C'est la vie, the gods laugh.
Not much you can do about it.
Enjoy it while you can.
Well, I am.
Here in my world,
doing
the Aztec two-step.

LEARNING CURVE

His first wife was, as they say, strong-willed.
He never should have married her
but you know how it is
one thing leads to another
they spend more and more time together
she starts picking out his ties
because, you know, he has no sense of style
and pretty soon
he's staring marriage in the face.

They finally got divorced, of course.
Now he's dating someone new.
She's not right for him either.
His first wife might have been a bitch
but she was right about one thing:
He has no sense of style.

THE DOLLHOUSE

They were the b-girls
the bar-girls, the party girls
who worked in certain bars,
would dance topless,
then would work the tables
asking if you'd like company
and if you said yes, they would sit down
and suddenly, as if by magic, a heavy matron
from behind the bar would appear at your table
asking, "Would you like to buy the lady a drink?"

These bars were almost always the same.
Some of the b-girl drinks cost fifty bucks
and had little to no alcohol
so it was always important to ask the price.

For every drink the b-girl sold
the matron would discretely give her
a small poker chip.
A different color depending on
the price of the drink she sold.
At the end of the evening the girls would exchange
their poker chips for cash, for their share.
That's how they got paid.
(That plus the dollars they made for stripping.)
So they kept you talking and they drank fast
and every time their glass was empty
the matron would magically appear.

There was no actual prostitution.
The matron wouldn't allow it.
The b-girl business was good,
so why screw it up with getting busted?

I met Amber at one of these places.
It was called the Dollhouse,
located in a sketchy section of town.

Amber was not a svelte girl
but she had energy when she danced
and so I slipped several dollars into her g-string
several times
and after her dance she came over to my table
and I smiled.
As she sat down, the matron appeared
and I ordered Amber a ten-dollar drink,
not the cheapest drink on the menu but
one that indicated I wanted her to stay and talk.

The first question out of Amber's mouth
was "Are you married?"
and, after a brief hesitation,
I told her I was
but that my wife was living in another state
(which was true—the divorce was in the works)
and Amber and I began to talk.

I visited the Dollhouse many times in those months
and I always sat with Amber.
After a while we started to date
and after a while we became lovers.

She told me all about her past.
She had to drop out of high school because
she was ADD and couldn't learn shit.
Her mom and younger sister lived in a trailer
outside of town.
Her mom collected some kind of disability.

She never mentioned a father.

She had a small apartment
and a cat with an eye infection.
I visited the apartment once.
It was filthy.
Clothes strewn everywhere,
litter box overflowing,
empty food containers,
complete disarray.
I was afraid to sit down
in case there were fleas.
She didn't have enough money
to take the cat to the vet
for its eye infection.

I don't know what she did with her money.
A lot of the Dollhouse girls did drugs
to keep their energy up on those long shifts.
Most of the girls started at 3:30 in the afternoon
when the construction crews let out,
and they didn't stop dancing, stripping, or talking
until the bar closed at 3:00 a.m.
I suspect Amber did drugs too.

Ours was an unusual relationship,
very easy going.
Many a night she would come to my apartment
at 3:30 in the morning
crawl into bed with me and fall asleep instantly.
I didn't mind.
In the morning when I left for work
she was dead to the world
in some deep deep dreamland.
God only knows what her dreams were like.

When we made love
she liked to be on top.
She would close her eyes
And rock back and forth
for as long I could hold on
and I would try to hold on
as long as I could.

She had the funniest sense of humor
of anyone I ever met.
Once I ran into her at a regular bar
and she ran up to me all excited.
"Roberto, buy me a drink, I'm celebrating!"
So I bought two beers at the bar
and brought them to the table where she was sitting.
"What are you celebrating?" I asked.
"I joined AA," she said, all proud of herself.

Eventually the drinking and drugs
and lack of money
got the best of her.
She left the Dollhouse
and joined an escort service
run by some other matron.

She and I drifted apart.
Well, that's not totally true.
She was doing more drugs,
was zoned out too much of the time
and the escort stuff bothered me,
so I started seeing less of her.

She called me one day all in tears
and came over to my apartment.

She had gotten herself pregnant
and had no money.
I made her some lunch while we talked.
As soon as I put the food on the table
she turned green, ran to the bathroom
and threw up.
I never knew her to lie to me before,
so I believed she was pregnant,
and the puking was sufficient proof for me.
I made the appointment for her
and drove her to the place that week
and paid for her abortion.

Time went by
I started a new job
and lost track of her.
The next year, I read her obituary in the local paper.
They listed her occupation as "artist."
In a sense, that was true.
I called up some old friends of hers
and asked what had happened.
She had overdosed, they told me.
Intentional or unintentional, no one knew.
I suspect it was a little of both.

What happens to these party girls
when the party's over?

There are so many Ambers—young energetic
talkative vivacious girls.
You know the ones, the center of attention,
the life of the party,
the ones who get a little too loud
when they're drunk
but no one minds because they're enchanted

by their looks, their mouths, their breasts,
the way they flip their hair, and the rest.
You know the ones:
The ones who talk about settling down
but never settle down,
The ones who are so verbally quick
but always in arrears.
They may have a job, but never a career,
Always on the verge of some new plan,
Always talking about finding the perfect man
but who never can.

You probably know one right now.
She's the one everyone wants to be with
tonight.

What happens to the party girls
when the party's over?

LINES

Lines that are used to begin certain letters:
> *I know it's been awhile since I've written*

Lines you never see anymore:
> *Here's the money I owe you*

Lines that give hope:
> *We really liked your manuscript*

Lines that dash hope:
> *We are unable at this time to*

Lines you wish you had written:
> *I really hate you*

Lines you wish you'd received:
> *I really love you*

Lines you're sorry you received:
> *I really need you*

Lines you never finished reading:
> *Let me tell you what I've done this year*

Lines you don't understand:
> *Why haven't you written?*

Lines you understand:
> *I'm sorry.*

Lines you will never write:
> *I've won the lottery!*

Lines you hope you will write:
> *I'm getting married!*

Lines you know you will write:
> *I'm sorry to tell you*

Lines you hope you never receive:
> *I'm sorry to tell you*

Lines that change things:
> *I need to tell you something*

Lines that matter:
> *Thank you so much*

NOT MUCH TO SAY

When it comes right down to it,
I don't have much to say,
Whatever happens, happens,
I don't have much to say.
Yes, I would like a new love
If one comes my way
Yes, I would like a free cruise
If I don't have to pay.
Yes, I would take off this mask
But don't ask me to do it fast
And yes I would like to dance
If I don't have to ask.
So what I'm saying is
When the rubber hits the road
When the going gets tough
When the rough get ready
And the ready get rough
And the situation is at the brink
And you turn to me and say
What do you think?
I will pour another drink and say
"Not much."

DOLLARS TO DOUGHNUTS

Lines written (while unemployed) in response to an email that said, "I bet you dollars to doughnuts they offer you that Commissioner's job."

well, to be honest
people like me don't get commissionerships
people like me
well, we jump off bridges
or work as public defenders
or go back to Oklahoma
or sell used cars
or become recluses
or disappear into a memory.
People like me
never make history
or appear in newspapers
or cut ribbons to open bridges.
People like me
are like xmas
are like easter
are like dawn,
after we're over
we're simply gone.
People like me
simply disappear
into smoke
into fog
into a memory.
People like me mail out resumes
in the morning
and buy box wine in the afternoon.
So here's a toast
to
people like me.

SHE HAS

She has intimations
of a perfectly free orgasm.
She has him
but his price is too high.
She has rocks that cost a moon shot.
He would like to shoot for the moon
but his feet are rocks
and she has
he has
she has a feeling
that soon hers will start too.

Planetoids off in the distance hum
like tiny birds.
She has tiny breasts that hum
when she dances to that rock and roll music.
He would like to roll off
onto some distant hay loft.
Straws stick in his back,
he's off on the wrong track
and she always brings herself back
too soon.
And she has intimations
of a perfectly free orgasm
perfectly seasonable
totally unreasonably
porpoise-like
she would like
a mad woman to be.
Asta Shasta Ruma Bovida
and she has.

TIME

Tick-tock
the bottle is empty
but if I open another
it will prove I need that drink
as opposed to merely desiring it.

Tick-tock
she is gone
I suppose I could call
and try and convince/cajole/swindle her back
but I simply don't have the energy...
I don't have the energy
or the desire
although desire is what first landed me on top of her
and inside her...
As that old song goes:
Desire just brings bruises...
well, when I say that old song
I mean, my secret song.

Tick-tock
I look in the mirror
and think, I might be able to pull this off one more year.
I use face cream now,
keep out of the sun,
still won't dye my hair.
I know a certain percentage of women are attracted to
older men...
a dwindling percentage
however
are attracted to old men.

Tick-tock

One more year
Tick-tock
One more year
Bring me more bottles
Bring me more women
Tick-tock.

COMMUNION

She was on the phone today
telling me about her blood test results
what the doctor said
what he didn't say
and I listen
to what she says
and to what she doesn't say.

She will get more test results tomorrow.
I tell her to call me when she does.
I know my function here
is to listen
while the horror unwinds its usual self.
There's nothing more I can do.

I was married to her for eight years
I've been divorced from her for seven years
She remarried.

I'm her only friend.

Odd how suffering brings people together.

THE HARDWAYS

I don't care what they say
growing old is horrible
sure, you think you know more
you don't
you think you're better off
you're not
you think you've worked out all the angles
you haven't

the only advantage
you tell yourself
is that your luck seems a little bit better
because you know how to avoid the obvious sucker bets
like the Big Six or the Big Eight
and it's true, you do avoid the meth-heads
at the end of the bar
the desperate recently divorced ones at work
you've learned how to avoid the unplanned weekend
you've learned how to structure the empty evenings
you've found the safe job
the quiet apartment
but you'll still bet on the Big Love
the worst hardway of all

I don't care what they say
the older you get
the more you're at the table
telling yourself you're not at the table
and the more you're at the table
the older you get

I "loaned" my girlfriend $2500
so she could get divorced.
Then she dumped me.

Tell me that wasn't the biggest sucker bet on the table.

REVISIONIST

odd...
finding a poem I had written late the night before
and not remembering that I wrote it
(there had been some drinking involved)
reading it
as if for the first time

It was about this woman I had met a few nights earlier

I decided to edit it a bit
take her name out
remove some of the more adolescent lines
make it sound like I wasn't such a fool

there
that's better

she was thirty years younger than me, after all,
and not interested in this old man

and I have to keep some dignity
even if it's after the fact.

THE IMPACT OF THE OPPOSITE

We used to have a saying
back when I worked in the mental hospital:
"the impact of the opposite is the same"
meaning that it didn't matter whether a parent beat you
or abandoned you—the impact on you was the same.

When Eve didn't call for a week
and then texted "I suppose I owe you an explanation,"
I texted back "not really."
Later when we met in the park
I could tell she really wanted to give me her reasons
for breaking up
I could tell she had rehearsed them
so she could mouth the words that implied she was taking responsibility
without taking responsibility, without saying I'm sorry.
But I told her I didn't need any explanation or reason.
What difference would it make?
The outcome was the same.
Besides, when someone is explaining why they did something
it's to obscure why they actually did it,
either from you or from themselves.

I was having lunch with this woman today
who was telling me how her and her fiancé had broken up
because she wanted to sleep with other men
and while they were broken up
his former girlfriend tricked him into sleeping with her
and then she (the former girlfriend) got pregnant
and so he married her.
I told her she was better off without him.
She cried, saying she still loved him.
I said that we often love people that are not good for us.

I don't work in mental hospitals anymore.
I got promoted to a bigger institution:
Relationships.

THE DAY OF REST

On Sunday mornings, I like to go to the bathhouse,
you know, take in a little steam,
relax in the heat amidst congenial company.

On Sunday mornings, the parking is plentiful and free
and there's few people on the street,
reducing the chance that someone I know
might see me slip into the bathhouse.
Once inside, I don't care who sees me
mi secreto es su secreto
and vice versa
and besides, it's very dark
and steamy inside.

Plus, it's cheap.
Twenty dollars buys me a small room for 8 hours
(I never stay more than 3)
a small room with a bed and a color TV
that plays a variety of porn.

I strip down, wrap a towel around me
and head for the showers
there's plenty of hot water
and soap
then into the steam room
with its dark corners.

You never know who you might meet.

After a few hours
I am relaxed
clean
purged of thought and worry
ready to face the week.

It's quite a thing, the bathhouse.

BUDDHA IS TURNING IN HIS GRAVE

You know,
I've almost got all the bases covered on this enlightenment thing:
Independent of root? *Check!*
Path is unknowable? *Check!*
Pasture is emptiness, signless, and free? *Check! Check! Check!*
Desire is throttled? Yeah... no, not so much.

I still haven't quite throttled all my desire.
Actually, I haven't throttled any of my desires.
I rather enjoy my desires.
I enjoy them more when they're being fulfilled, of course,
but even when they're hungry,
even when my tongue is longing
for that soft flesh
or for that hard flesh
Even when my mouth is starving,
I enjoy my desires.

Even when I'm sitting alone at the bar
down to my last dollar
leafing through the ads for escorts
in the local underground paper
even then
I'm enjoying my desires.

I am so close on this enlightenment thing.

But let's face it,
enlightenment is good
but it can't hold a candle to good fucking.

Desire is more than the gift of God—
It's God in the flesh.

THE OUTSIDER

I feel like such a misfit,
meaning, I don't fit in anywhere.
It's not that I don't know what to do
in any given situation,
I always know exactly what I'm supposed to do
in any given situation.
It's just that I don't want to do what I'm supposed to do
in any given situation.

Every situation feels like some foreign film that I'm watching
and not understanding the language
and the subtitle keeps repeating
"You don't belong here, buddy."

For example (and there are so many examples):
last week Herlinda texted me and asked,
"Do you want to meet for a beer one day after work?"
and I reply "Absolutely"
and then I ask "Are you going to the wine meet-up tonight at 9 pm?"
and she texts back, "No, I don't stay up that late"
so I text back, "Ok, but yes on the beer get-together. Just pick a day"
and I never hear from her again.

Now I know what she wanted me to do.
She wanted me to text back, "Absolutely, let's do it today."
Making me the dom, the mover of the action, the one who is inviting her
even though she initiated the contact.
But I don't want to be that guy
I'm not interested in pursuing her
though I would bed her in a minute.
Maybe that's the odd part.

Being an outsider
is a subtle art.

Herlinda is kind of a negative person.
I've drank with her before.
She's sort of hard to talk with
but I know she's lonely and not with anyone.
She probably didn't want to risk rejection
She didn't want to "pick a day"
because that makes her the dom, the mover of the action
and she doesn't want to be that person
either.

I don't ever remember feeling like I belonged anywhere.

So later that same day,
I'm getting ready to go to the wine meet-up
and I get a text from Eve
and she asks "Are you going to the gay pride parade tomorrow?
Would you like to grab a cup of coffee and chat for a bit?"
And I text back that I didn't have any plans
other than going to work (on a Saturday) but yes,
text me in the morning and we can get together for coffee.
And she texts back that she is "feeling overwhelmed"
by her new job
And misses filtering with me.
(Of course, she broke up with me, but I don't point that
fact out to her.)
And I text back, "Ok, well, text me tomorrow
and we'll get together,"
and she texts back "Ok, thank you.... You are a good guy."

Now I know what she wants me to do:
she wants me to act concerned, maybe alarmed,

ask if she wants to get together tonight.
She wants me to listen to her emotions,
to commiserate, to offer advice, counsel, support,
but you know
I didn't create her problem
with her job

I suspect tomorrow that she will intimate
we should get back together.
I know what any other man would do
she's a beauty
and I used to love her so much
but now I just feel detached
maybe that's more realistic,
I don't know...
but I won't get back together with her.

So I head off to the wine meet-up.
There's a band, and they're pretty good
and a bar, so I get a drink.
The bartender is a woman named Kat, probably short for Katrina.
I think she's attractive.
She knows me and my drinking habits.
She used to serve me and Eve when we drank there.
I like Kat, but I can never get past her personification
her presentation,
her role as bartender
so I order a glass of wine and check out the crowd
I see two women from the wine meet-up at a table.
They do not recognize me, which is good
because I do not like them.
I have talked with them before.
They sit with each other and do not dance.

The band is playing and they are good.
Many people are dancing
but they are mostly young
well, younger than me.
So I stand in a dark corner and observe.

Now I know what I should do:
I should go dance.
People are just in the crowd dancing,
not dancing with anyone in particular, just dancing,
or I should go ask one of the many women sitting at tables
to dance,
but I don't.

I don't know if there is something wrong with me
or something very right with me.

But the band is good, and I enjoy them
and I enjoy watching the people dance
but I also feel like I'm watching that foreign film again.

I finish my drink and wander out into the cool night air.
There is music everywhere tonight.
I walk down a few blocks to Rumours Bar,
a place I like.
It's a tiny wine bar.
Veronica the owner is there.
I like her.
She's older but attractive.
I've talked with her many times.
The bar is her first business venture.
It's empty (on a Friday night!) except for Veronica's mother
who comes there to keep Veronica company
in these lean times.

I know what I should do.
I should go in and have a glass of wine, show my support,
chat with Veronica,
see if there's any way I could eventually bed her.
But I don't.
I walk by.

I decide to give the dance one more chance
(after all, I paid a $15 cover)
so I go back, show my stamped hand, get waved in,
go up to Kat and order another glass of wine.
People are still dancing
The song is good
but then it ends
and the band announces it is taking a break.

I know what I should do.
I should simply wait until intermission is over
maybe try and talk to someone
simply wait for more dancing opportunities
after all, dancing is life,
and after all, I just got this glass of wine
and have only had a few sips.
But I don't.
I put the full glass down and walk out
into the cool night air.

All my life
I have never belonged
anywhere.

No complaints—it's just a fact.

So tomorrow, I will go to work for a while.

Eve will text.
I will join her for coffee.
She will tell me how tough it is,
how she is so confused.
Maybe I'll get a text from Jane
telling me how tough it is for her
and how she misses me too...

If I had a nickel for every time I heard some woman say
she thought I was a nice guy and missed me...

Sunday I think I will go to the gay bathhouse
and take in some steam
to clear my thoughts.

I know what others expect me to do
I just don't do it
I just don't care anymore
I just don't fit in anywhere.

VOYEUR

Ha.
In the apartment across the street
on the second floor, eye level to me,
through the window I see
a man and a woman, sitting,
talking to each other.
She is talking, gesturing.
Now he is talking.
She leans forward
elbows on the table
head down.
He continues talking.
Now she holds her head in both her hands.

Now she is talking very fast
and gesturing rapidly.
He is leaning back
arms across his chest.

I'll bet this will go on for quite a while.
That's the problem with relationships:
There's always something to work out.

I turn my attention to my wine glass
Almost empty
Luckily there's another bottle.

No accusatory words here,
Nothing to work out,
Just another pleasant evening
with me and my silent friend:
Al K. Hall

CURIOUS

What's wrong
with simply being curious?
With wanting to have sex with someone just once,
just to see what it's like,
just because
you're curious?

Why can't there be a free sample
like they do at the ice cream shop?
If I like the coconut lemon custard,
I'll order the whole cone.
If not, I'll order something else.

Ah, but suppose the coconut lemon custard
wants you more than you want it?
What if it starts texting you, emailing you,
dropping by unannounced?
That's a problem.
I don't want to open my door and find
a huge jaded and crazed coconut lemon custard cone.

On the other hand
If you only hang around the NSA websites
and sex clubs
you become jaded and crazed yourself.
And so, you strike the middle course:
You hang around the NSA websites
and the sex clubs
but you also go to the meet-ups, the gymnasiums,
the afterwork get-togethers,
hoping to find someone who's not jaded and crazed
but merely curious herself.

It's a mysterious dance:
To appear respectable
While seeking carnal.

REPUBLICANS

I was dating this Republican
(it's a long story)
and I had bought this silver bracelet
twisted in the shape of barb wire
it was quite creative
and I was wearing it on my left wrist
next to my watch.

This Republican and I had gone on vacation together
and I had a small stone from a beach we had visited
and I wanted to commemorate our vacation
and have the stone put into a necklace
for me to wear
and she and I were at an outdoor farmers' market
and there was a silversmith there
and I negotiated a deal with the silversmith
to make me a necklace
for this stone
to commemorate our vacation
together.

And I was feeling pleased with myself
for finding this silversmith
and as we walked away from his booth
I mentioned to my Republican girlfriend
that in 18 months I would become vested
in the pension plan at work
and I was going to commemorate that occasion
by getting my ear pierced
(or re-pierced actually, but that's another long story)
and she said,
and I quote,

"Be careful. If you wear that bracelet and the necklace and the earring, people might think you're gay."

Now, some nice young man
whose name I didn't catch
had just sucked me off at the bathhouse the week before, but that was not the kind of thing that I wanted to mention to my Republican girlfriend at that moment, so I just said, "Yeah, you're probably right."

BREAKING EVEN

my girlfriend broke up with me
my boss called in sick
I won $5 on a $5 scratch ticket
my test results came back negative
the company I work for decided not to lay anyone off
I was able to cover my rent
I have just enough wine for tonight.

I mailed out some more poems and
got a rejection letter from the last mailing
in the same day.

There's enough gas in the car
to make it to work tomorrow and back.
There a bit of cash in my wallet and the weekend ahead.
I'm up to date on my bills and my correspondence.

I get no phone calls,
no texts, no emails.

My therapist asks me no questions
The liquor store always takes my checks.

I don't have a date for the weekend
but the gay bathhouse is open.

You see, everything balances out
or as they say in tennis
the score is
love love.

THE MATERIALIZATION AND VAPORIZATION OF THOUGHT ITSELF

Every night is October thirty-first
You know the time of year,
El Día de los Muertos,
Halloween, All Saints Day,
the time when the veil between the two worlds is the thinnest.
Ghosts speak to me at night.
The number of ghosts is incalculable
infinite
crammed into my dreams.
I bring back fresh knowledge every morning
like honeydews cleaved in half,
the small seeds scooped out.
The green flesh glistens in the sun.
By noon I am dumb.
Every night is October thirty-first
the time when the two worlds join and separate
join and separate
join and separate
like heartbeats
like lovers.

WHAT HAPPENS TO THESE WOMEN?

I'll try to make some sense of this.
I was sitting in Rumours Bar
a favorite haunt of mine
and an older lady comes in
and takes the seat furthest away from me.

There's this jazz guitarist playing in the bar
softly, but very well.
It's one of the reasons I like the bar.
They have good taste in music
and they have wine
and I'm on my third or fourth drink.

Rumours is in a building
with a hair salon,
and through the full side window I can watch
people getting their hair cut,
blown dry, curled, colored, etc.
Out the front window I can see
the parade of horrors on the sidewalk
the homeless, the strange, the beautiful.

The woman at the end of the bar is not beautiful.
She is probably younger than me (everyone is) but
she is overweight, dumpy, with flabby arms
her hair is dyed brown but her double chin tells her age.
She keeps looking at me.

The jazz guitarist is very good.
He wears a wedding ring.

Across the way in the salon window
I watch a woman who works there.

Her hair is dyed blond
but she is young.
She is wearing a blouse that falls off one shoulder
exposing a bra strap.
I watch her.

An older woman comes in to have her hair styled.
The blond chats with her.
The older woman's hair is obviously dyed brown.
The blond washes it, puts some conditioner in it.
They chat.
I look at the older woman in the salon chair.
She is simply not pretty.
A jutting chin, thin lips, it's a harsh look.
I don't mean to be judgmental
but I am.
I would not fuck her.

That's the criteria for men, you know:
Would I fuck her?
They say that women need a reason to have sex
while men just need a place,
but that's not the whole story.
There are some women that we (or at least I) will not fuck.
What happens to these women?

So I watch the blonde put conditioner in the older woman's hair
and the older woman is running her hands through her hair
to help spread the conditioner around.
and she watches herself in the mirror
and leans her head back and flips her hair
for maximum penetration...
... maximum penetration.

After a few minutes the blonde comes back and blow-dries
the woman's hair
then cuts it a little
then styles it.
It does look better
but I still would not fuck her.

The older woman leaves the salon.
The blonde checks her cell phone.
Is she waiting for a message?
What's her life?

An older man comes in and negotiates a transaction.
The blonde begins to give him a pedicure.
His feet soaking in warm water.
She is sitting lower than him
exposing cleavage
working on his feet.
He is obviously enjoying this
but she is avoiding any eye contact with him,
keeps looking around
only responds when he asks her questions.
He thinks he's an ancient Roman being attended to
by some blonde slave.
But he's just another customer to her,
another dollar.
So she bends forward to cut his toenails
as he looks down her blouse
and I do as well.

He is clearly relishing his role as the centurion
having a pedicure.
While his feet soak some more,
She checks her cell phone.

The older woman at the end of the bar
orders another drink
and continues to look at me.

The guitarist continues to play
miraculously well
amazingly well
I am the only one listening
the only one clapping my hands after every song.

Outside there is a steady stream of
mostly fat people, lumbering along the boulevard
in front of Rumours.
Who fucks fat people? I want to know.
BBW aside, how do they actually get their needs met?

My last girlfriend used to call me up and say:
"My vagina is hungry."
Her vagina was hungry very often,
and I was pleased to feed it.
She was no freak—just honest.

I look at these fat women, these dumpy women
these flabby armed, obese, thick, double-chinned women
who never exercise
(and let me tell you, going to a class three times a week is
not exercise)
and who are younger than me
and I wonder,
who feeds their hungry vaginas?

I know the answer: No one does.
It's the secret that older women carry
and do not share,
not even with each other.

No one fucks them anymore.
So they dye their hair
and they go to bars
and they wait
for something that will never happen again.

I think about this as I order another glass of wine
and listen to the jazz guitarist.
Did I mention he was very good?
I'll plug his name
just because he was so good:
Tarik Bentemsani.

The man getting the pedicure leaves.
The blonde checks her cell phone again.
She never calls or texts anyone,
she only checks for messages.
Evidently, there are none.

Another older man comes in for a haircut.
I can tell he is affluent by his hairstyle.
(Odd, how that is.)
He chats with the blond
I can tell there is flirting and cajoling back and forth.
She cuts his hair.
It seems like a good haircut.
Still, he is twice her age, maybe more.

(I have been in that position myself.)

He leaves. She counts her tips. The real truth.
It is the end of her shift. She packs up her things and
leaves.

I wonder where she goes. Is she married? Living with someone?
But of course, I'll never know.

The guitarist continues to play.
The woman at the end of the bar sits alone
and steals glances at me.

It's another drunken evening for me.
I buy a CD from the guitarist, tip him $10,
pay my tab and head out into the street.

Who fucks older fat women?
Is this sacrilege to ask?
I certainly have had my share of lovers who were "curvy" or simply big women,
but they were different.
They weren't flabby or out of shape,
Hell, they often wore me out.

But now I see older women lumber like hippos on the sidewalk,
sweating, huffing and puffing, thick haunches moving like some Tyrannosaurus Rex
and I wonder,
who feeds their hungry vaginas?

LIFE

Herbert on his bicycle pedals along
the sky is grey
he disappears around the corner
as if he was never here.

No food before the ultrasound
no partaking of bread
certainly no wine.
I stretch out on the altar.
Dr. Abraham walks in.

I did laundry last night
or was it the night before?
or did I do it at all?
I don't remember.

We're all murderers and prostitutes.
My ex-wife married a rich old man
hoping he would die soon
now eight years later he's still around
but bankrupt.
Now they live off her money.

I look around and suddenly it's tomorrow.
I'll get my test results by noon.
Herbert pedals by again.
Now he's gone.

MEET AND GREET

The local (secret) sex club is throwing a meet-and-greet tomorrow,
a party "for people seeking new partners for play, sex or dating."

Most of the people who go to this sex club are couples into BDSM.
They hold weekly meetings at the club
where they flog each other,
tie each other to posts,
occasionally enact rape scenes.
I go and watch sometimes.
It's very entertaining.

There are also transgender parties, and queer parties
at this sex club.
They provide a great public service.

I've been a member for 5 years
but I've never met anyone there,
never participated in any event.

I go to their parties, find a comfortable place to sit
and wait.
Occasionally a hostess in a leather corset comes by
and asks if I'm doing alright, if I'm having fun
I always answer in the affirmative
even though it's not true.

According to the website, there will be customizable name tags
at the meet-and-greet tomorrow night
to make it easy to find what you're looking for.
What would mine say?
Hello, I'm Roberto
I'm looking for love.
Complete, utter, total, carnal, love.

I suppose I could just write "slave."
I'm a slave to love.

Well, no matter.
I will go.

I will find a comfortable place to sit and watch.
And after awhile, I will leave
unobserved
and head over to the gay bathhouse
for some real relief.

IAGO

Ali in the apartment downstairs
Is 25 years younger than me
Vivacious, fleshy, exotic, exuberant,
but like I say, 25 years younger than me
but she's having trouble with her boyfriend Eduardo.
I listen attentively to her dilemma,
and encourage her to give him another chance
knowing the relationship is doomed
(he's an idiot)
hoping I can catch her right at that point
after the break-up
before the next boyfriend
when she is lonely
and horny
maybe take her out for a consolatory drink
or two or three or four...

Hoping I can bed her down
and open those secret places
once
or twice

Knowing she will find another boyfriend after that
because she is, as I say,
young and pretty.

That's how it is with us old Lotharios:
We take our pleasures when we can

Infrequent as they may be.

SOMEONE FOR EVERYONE

They say there's someone for everyone
and judging from who my friends marry
I guess that's true.

The women I've known who were beautiful,
Exuberant, vivacious, creative,
married older, fat, arrogant, rich men
who bullied and belittled them until
the women lost their beauty, their creativity,
their energy.

The men I've known who were decent,
caring, intelligent, humorous, independent,
married controlling demanding shrill women
who nagged and extorted them until
the men lost all their humor, all their independence.

The only marriages I've seen where the partners
have kept their humanity, their spark, their love,
their independence and sense of humor
have been the open marriages
(and not all of those have worked).

Still, in a secret place in my heart
I keep that crazy hope alive
that somewhere out there...

Well, you know that secret, don't you?

You have it too.

SOBRIETY

Well, I'm giving my liver a rest I guess,
eleven days now without a drink
and I'm exercising more
and I've lost four pounds
and I sleep better
and I don't arrive at work hung-over
and my side (the side where my liver is)
doesn't hurt
and I'm saving money every night
by not going to bars
and by not buying cases of wine
for home consumption,
and I'm no longer falling down drunk
or waking up not remembering exactly
what I did
or what I wrote the night before
and my face doesn't looked bloated
and haggard in the morning mirror
and I seem to be making more conversation
at work
and my life and my daily schedule
have a rationality
that is new to me.

I hope I detoxify soon
so I can go back to drinking
because I am bored to fucking death.

SOME OF THE TIME

Walking through the city streets
one sees many things that make you think.
Here's a petite bleach blond with a guy in a muscle t-shirt
emerging from a motel room.
I think of all the women emerging with a guy
from some motel room
and imagine that some of them, not all of them,
but some of them, spent the night fucking.

It's like this girl once told me
when I asked her to describe the perfect date
and she said, "He would fly me to Vegas
and we'd spend the entire weekend either fucking
or hanging out at the pool."
(I didn't disagree with her—it does sound nice.)
It's funny to think of girls thinking like men
wanting to spend all day fucking
and I imagine that some of them, not all of them,
but some of them, do…
on occasion… maybe.

I remember staying in a motel once
where the walls were quite thin
and the couple next door were fucking for a long time
and he kept saying, "Okay let's try it this way"
and there would be a pause
and then the pounding would start again
and after about an hour he started asking
"Did you come yet?"
(I wondered if he was getting tired.)
I heard all this because I had my ear pressed against
the wall.
The next morning I saw them in the lobby

bleach blond in a mini skirt
and he obviously lifted weights
young, self-absorbed, vacant.

Walking through the city streets
one sees many things that make you think.
A woman is setting out tables and umbrellas
for the brunch crowd.
She has many chairs to move around.
She looks up at me as I walk by
and then goes back to her chairs
and I wonder if women think about sex
when they are doing other things
like moving chairs.
Guys do,
or at least, I do.

Walking through the park
where many joggers are starting their day
with a run.
Some because it's healthy
Some because it's habit
Some because they have to
to keep looking attractive.
The guys just wear any old pair of shorts
and a t-shirt, but the girls have color-coordinated
tank tops, shoes, short-shorts, and barrettes.
Maybe women are so trained to dress up
that they pick fashionable jogging outfits out of habit.
But I suppose some of them run so they can meet men
while they are running.
Maybe some actually do.

Walking through the city streets
one sees many things that make you think.

And what I think is that I really know nothing.
I have no idea what people do
how often they achieve their perfect dates
their perfect jogging hook-ups
their perfect motel stays.
All that stuff stays behind locked doors
where it belongs.
It's probably better that way
because no matter what the truth is,
it would be depressing.

THANK YOU MICHAEL MALYSZKO

There's a photograph in my bathroom
hanging right over the toilet
so that I am at eye level with it
every time I pee
so I can enjoy it
every time I pee
and I do enjoy it.

It is a photograph of two people in bed.
The boy is young, maybe 17 or 18, and fast asleep.
He is lean, slightly muscular, has a tattoo
around his left bicep
clean cut
waxed chest
sheet draped over his lower torso
sleeping mouth open
sexy, handsome but not bright looking.
The woman is older. 45? 50? 55?
Attractive, well preserved, well made-up,
sheet covering a carefully maintained voluptuous body
smiling contented, staring into space
smoking a cigarette
her right hand absent-mindedly stroking
the boy's hair.

The furniture in the bedroom is expensive.
The accessories are feminine.
The room is hers and she is wealthy.

They are clearly naked under the sheets and
they've obviously just had sex.
Two empty glasses by the bed
next to an open bottle of Johnny Walker Red

bra and underwear thrown across the back
of a nearby chair.
The smoke from her cigarette floats lazily upward.
She looks very contented, very happy.

But the impact of the photograph is the
difference in their ages
the wonderfulness of that moment pitted against
the impossibility of an extended future together.
The impact of the photograph is the brevity of bliss.
And bliss it is
while he sleeps
and she relives the lovemaking, and glows.

The photograph was taken by Michael Malyszko
a professional photographer.
I found it in a trade book of photographers' agents
a book full of sample photographs of so many
great photographers
but this one I liked the best
so I cut it out and framed it.

After a year or so I decided to tell Mr. Malyszko
how much pleasure his photograph had brought me.
I found his email in the book (which I still had)
and emailed him my thanks.
To my surprise he emailed back that week
and we corresponded a bit.
He told me the scene took a while to set up,
that the boy really had fallen asleep
and that the woman was a former Playboy model
all of which only added to my pleasure.

So few pieces of art actually capture life
capture the impossibility of it

capture the essence of those brief stolen moments
that we stumble into and greedily devour
and hope we can hold on to
but never can.
They slip away from us like the smoke
that lilts upward from her cigarette.

Like a camera obscura, that photograph is projected
through my eyes onto the faces and bodies
of every woman and every man I meet.

WHAT LOVE IS

When I say I love you
I mean
there's some aspect of you that excites me enough
to make me overlook the parts of you that are disagreeable.
For example,
the sex with Sherri was so hot
she could just take her clothes off and
I would get the fever just looking at her.
Then I could never keep my hands off her.
There wasn't a nook or cranny of her body
that my tongue or my cock did not explore.
I devoured her every time she came over,
but
we never had anything to talk about
she couldn't hold a conversation of more than
three sentences.
When she finally went back to her husband
I was devastated, heart-broken, ruined, destroyed.
Later, much later, I was just grateful.

Here's another example,
I never met a woman who could make me laugh more
than Trigger.
We made each other laugh til we choked.
Our dinners together were filled with funny stories,
Puns, daring flirtations, wild intellectual dialogues.
Hanging out with her was pure joy.
The sex was pretty good too, not mind blowing,
but pretty damn good.
And all of that was good enough to make me overlook
the fact that she was totally irresponsible.
She kept these two huge dogs in a one bedroom apartment,
couldn't/wouldn't train them
would take them out for a walk without poop bags

and take off their leashes claiming she could control them,
and of course, they would break free
shitting on all the irate neighbors' yards
disappearing up the streets
she'd get frantic, unhinged, crying,
running down the streets calling their names
"Berkley, Jacky" at the top of her lungs.
This was an everyday occurrence.
Or she could call me up in the middle of the night
lost on some freeway because she didn't bring a map
crying because she hadn't eaten all day
and I'd have to talk her down
navigate her home like a damaged aircraft
with a blind pilot
then I'd drive over to her place
pick up a pizza on the way
just to have food ready when she arrived.
Noblesse oblige of love I told myself.
She was a mess.
I was in love.

When she left me
I was devastated, heart-broken, ruined, destroyed.
Later, of course, I was just grateful.

The list goes on and on.
Something about the other person
excites us, makes our nerve endings light up
like sparklers in the dark of our lonely nights
and we want that heat, that fire, that sex,
that madness, that laughter, that joy, that connection
so we ignore the fact
that our fingers are burning.

I'm not condemning that madness.
I'd do it all again
In fact, I will do it again, I'm sure.
It's the closest I'll ever get to love.

COSTUME PARTY

There's a carnival down by the harbor this week
within walking distance of my little apartamento
and it's a fine evening for walking.
The sun stays up late on these lazy summer evenings
so I head down there.
I am wearing my old man costume.
You know the look:
straw panama hat, sunglasses,
polo shirt, leather sandals.
It's a sensible outfit.
That's one of the marks of age:
sensibility.

The crowd is mostly teenagers and pre-teens,
not quite so sensible.
The girls have discovered the power of
sexuality
and they all wear the same costume:
short-shorts (cut right to the crotch)
tank tops or see-through blouses with
black bras,
hair piled on top of their heads,
mostly bleach blond heads,
some with wild streaks of red or blue,
a multitude of bracelets
and often, a multitude of tattoos.
These are the pre-teens and early teenagers.
The twenty-year olds are pushing baby carriages.
Odd how that works.

The thirty and forty year olds are conspicuously absent
and probably at the bars,
which is where I should be

(but my doctor has told me
to give my liver a rest for a bit
and I, being a sensible man, am following his advice
for a few weeks).

The boys at the carnival are all in the same costume
regardless of age:
white t-shirts with the sleeves cut off,
long baggy shorts.

I notice that there are few hat-wearers
despite the evening sun
but my dermatologist has advised me
to wear a hat
and I, being a sensible man,
follow his advice.

I walk through the carnival and check out the games.
They haven't changed since my childhood.
Toss the basketball through the secretly too-small hoop
to win a prize
or pop the under-inflated balloon with the blunt-tip dart
to win a prize
or knock over all three of the secretly weighted bottles
with a baseball
to win a prize.
And the prizes look good hanging on the carny tent
but if you actually get one home
you soon find
they are never quite as good as you thought.
Not that much different than life.
Work three more years to get vested
and win a fast-disappearing pension.
Wine and dine that woman in accounting
for three months

to discover how boring she
(or you)
really is.
Sometimes just the act of getting up and going to work
or just the act of talking to people
feels like being the yokel at the carnival.

But I digress.

I think I was talking about
being dressed like an old man
and walking around the carnival,
and by the way
when you're in the old man costume at the carnival
you are invisible to anyone younger.
They simply do not see you.
You move like a ghost among them.
You have to walk around them
as they do not sense your presence,
absorbed as they are with wanting to play the games.
They stand in the midway of life,
completely mesmerized by the sight and sound
of the games, the colors, the prizes, the razzle-dazzle.
They block the midway as they stand there
in groups, all with their mouths open.

Not that much different than life.

Oh, I see I have digressed again.
That's another mark of age, you know.
Everything reminds you of what a horrible
wasted pointless sham everything is
and so, one tends to digress a bit.

Anyway, I found the carny food wagons

and bought a cheeseburger (for $8)
and found a place to sit down
where I could eat comfortably and still watch
the crowd.
The cheeseburger was pretty good
and the people flowed around me the way the water
flows around a large boulder
in the middle of the river.
I ate slowly just so I could linger
and watch the endless swirls and eddies of people
all different all the same
like the ever changing foam in the same river water
all the same costumes all the different shapes
all merging talking babbling as they flowed by me.
I found myself feeling some odd kinship
with this river
the way one feels at the dog pound
when one sees so many caged animals,
too many to save,
and one feels a type of pity that almost feels like love.

Ah, well, I see I have digressed again.
That's the last mark of age you know:
sentimentality.

Sorry about that.
Things will be better when my doctor tells me
it's okay to drink again.

ON THE WAIT

The young man sits on his towel
and leans against the wall
of the steam room
one leg stretched out on the tile
the other hanging over the edge
of the tier where he lingers.
Droplets of water hang from his pubic hairs
like dew on the morning grass.
The steam hisses and half obscures him.

Men, mostly older and heavier, walk slowly by,
eyeing him,
eyeing his face, his lean body, his cock.
They look for a sign.
One or two of the bolder men brush their hand
over the leg that hangs over the edge,
looking for a response.
He gives none and they move on.

He is waiting for someone to walk by,
someone who sparks something indefinable,
that click of attraction.

The young woman sits at the bar with her girlfriend.
They are talking about their day, fashion, gossip,
sipping at drinks and nibbling at appetizers.
Men walk by trying to catch her eye,
looking for a sign.
One or two of the bolder men say something
rehearsed but witty.
She smiles, brushes them off,
and returns to her conversation.
Yet she is actually there waiting

for someone to walk by
someone who will spark that something indefinable,
that click of attraction.
This is how it is.

We are all in the bar
or in the steam room
or on the boat
in the lake
or on the rebound
or on the make
but mostly
we're on the wait
waiting for someone to walk in
waiting for the tumblers to fall
exactly right
in some genetically prescribed pattern
the curse of natural selection
that makes the eggs fall
and fans the erection.

BELOW THE SURFACE

Poetry is nice, I guess, but life is more complicated.
Things are never what they seem to be.
Take for instance my neighbor, Sarah.
29 years old, nice girl, good looking...
(But she's half my age, alas,
and so we don't date because she thinks
I'm too old for her, but we are good friends).
She has a steady job working for a good company,
educated, has a Master's degree, speaks a second language,
interesting to talk to, seems to have a level head.
Well... she tells me that one time
about 3 years ago
when she and her ex-boyfriend were low on money
they decided (and it was her idea)
that she would turn a trick for cash
so she perused Craigslist
and found an ad from some married man
with the usual double entendres about
being generous,
and she emailed him.
and because she had never done this before
she did take precautions,
met him at a casino first
and made arrangements for her "date"
to occur on the following week.
He was to take her out to dinner
and then back to his hotel
and he would pay for her dinner
plus give her $300 for sex afterwards.
According to Sarah he was nice enough looking
but arrogant, kept telling her he was a "great lover"
and would make her come.
Made her promise "not to fall in love with him"

because the last one, he claims, did
and then called his house
and his wife found out,
and he swore to his wife that he would never
do this again.
Anyway, to make a long story short,
Sarah met him for dinner the following week
(kept a cell phone in her purse to keep in touch
with her boyfriend who was monitoring the "date")
and after dinner Sarah told the man the price
would be $400, not $300.
The man balked, but eventually gave in.
They went back to his hotel
and he fucked her.
She pretended it was great
but of course she was just doing it for the money.

Sarah tells me the story matter-of-factly
and I listen and accept what she says
without judgment
because I do not have any judgments about such things.
I accept the things that people do
magnanimously.
No behavior is foreign to me.
I smile and compliment her on her creativity
and tuck the story away
for the day
when I have
an extra
$400
lying around.

I SUPPOSE NORMAL PEOPLE
MAKE NORMAL WEEKEND PLANS

I'm making a list for tomorrow.
If I leave at 10 a.m., I'll get to the city by noon.
The strip club opens at 11:00—I can have lunch there.
They serve a decent cheeseburger.
Get a least one lap dance,
some soft breasts rubbed in my face,
maybe even a mouth of fur and
a touch of labia on my chin
feel firm thighs wrapped around my legs.
That would get me properly primed.
After awhile I'll head up the street to the gay bathhouse.
I should get there by 2:00.
By then there's should be some folks there.
I'll get a room with a video with lots of porn,
take a nice steam,
slide naked into the hot tub full of men
soak for a while
see who sits close to me
see who rubs his hands over my thigh.
Maybe I'll lie naked on the enclosed sun deck
see who approaches me
and weigh carefully what they want
(because safety is my number one goal,
alongside anonymity).

If I time it right, I should be home by 5:00
and when my neighbors ask me what I've been up to
I'll just say, "not much"
and see if they want to grab a beer.

WHEN WE WERE LOVERS

oh look
there she is
my former lover
my former almost-fiancée
my my
she is looking good
but somehow not as heart-stopping gorgeous
as when we were lovers
oh she is speaking to me...
yes? yes?
she tells me she is moving this weekend
away from that little apartment she took 6 months ago
to be near me
the one we used to make love in
when we were lovers
back when
I loved her so much
so deeply
now she is moving out of that little apartment
okay
she doesn't volunteer where she is moving to
and I don't ask
but I do think I know
I would bet she is moving back in with her husband
the one she left
so that she and I could become lovers
either that or she kicked him out of the house
and she is moving back into the empty house
and if that's the case, I predict he'll work his way
back into the house eventually
after all, they've been married for 24 years
and that's how people are, you know
people basically don't, or won't, change their ways

they won't change their habits
people just repeat the same pattern over and over
and if that's true for them,
then it's true for me
but the positive side is
that means I can look forward to many more
passionate lovers
and almost fiancées
who will leave me to return
to their husbands.

And now I know that when they say
they want a no-strings-attached relationship
it just means that I will be left
with a lot of loose ends.

GROOMING BEHAVIOR

This may sound gross I know,
but one of my ex-wives, for some reason,
liked to squeeze the blackheads on my back.
You know, the hard little ones that you can't reach yourself.
About once a week, she would say to me
"Roll over, let me check your back."
And she would really get into it
cleaning out the pores and
dabbing them with alcohol.

These private grooming behaviors are
what makes a marriage special,
what keeps a couple together
like how monkeys preen each other, looking for fleas
and, I have to admit, it was very relaxing.
It endeared her to me.

The marriage failed for other reasons,
but when I think back
to the things I miss about being married to her
I have to admit
that little ritual was near the top of the list.

I don't think she was unique in liking to do that.
I was at a brothel once in Tennessee
where this lovely Korean lady,
before fucking me,
noticed my back and made me lie on my stomach
while she did the same thing—squeezed the blackheads—
then she fucked me.
It made the fucking almost tender
as if we were married
and loved each other.

THE CALIBER OF A PERSON

Today I read about some rampage in Florida
where someone shot seven people dead
and the newspaper had the usual quotes
from the neighbors.
"He was a loner."
"We didn't know him well."
"He kept to himself."
"He rarely spoke."

Although one woman said more.
She said, "I knew from the look in his face
that he had been alone for a long time."

I went and checked my face in the mirror
and made a mental note to try
and talk with more people.

KARMA

I don't believe in past lives
I don't think I was a conquistador
or a king
or a slave
or anything like that in some past life.

I don't believe in a future life
either on earth or in heaven
I don't think I'll be given wings
or burn in hell or come back as some unknown bodhisattva.

I do, however, believe in the present life
that I am king over my thoughts
and slave to my desires
and like some mad Ponce de Leon
I too search for the lost fountain of youth
and I most certainly am an unknown bodhisattva
trying to show myself the way.
These bureaucratic hallways are my endless villages
these pointless meetings where I wander
these meaningless charts on tracking accountability
and creating the parameters of change
and other babble of minds stuck in cause and effect.
I look around the table and see my fellow slaves
in this galley ship rowing towards retirement
unable to remove our chains
that we ourselves have forged.
I preach the unknowable path to my own deaf ears.

Who needs past lives to learn from?
All our stories are right here right now.
The murders, the crown, the failed marriages, the carnage,
the chance, the opportunity, the ignorance, the repetition.

Here I am right now
repeating my past into my future
right now.

WHAT A PIECE OF WORK

For those of us who live
amongst these creatures,
for those of us who live quietly
amongst these silent mollusks of men
while overfed and opinionated women
glide above and around us,
for those of us who forage silently
in the coral,
working our jobs, knowing our place
in the ecology of capitalism,
taking our cut and recycling the rest,
darting through the kelp,
keeping our little thoughts a secret,
keeping our eyes open at all times
while drifting with the currents,
for those of us who endure in solitude,
finding hidden places to rest
and more hidden places to spawn,
we know this secret.

We, the paragon of animals,
born and bred in illusion,
are caricatures of evolution,
upside down and underwater
in more ways than one,
sold down the river,
surviving only by collusion,
no better than eels.

Those of us who live
amongst these creatures
know this secret.

EMBLEMS

It's funny how some relationships get summarized
in one succinct memory,
say, of one particular afternoon or one particular moment,
like when Terese turned to me
as we were leaving my apartment and asked
with a smile, "Do I look freshly fucked?"

Or sometimes it's the bad memories that
get seared into your brain,
like when Jane announced she was leaving me
and I just sat there on the couch and looked at her
and then she spat out,
"See? I knew you'd have nothing to say."

All those weeks, months, or years, of a relationship
get distilled down to one memory
like the way we remember that one scene from some
movie we've long forgotten.

I was married to my first wife for eleven years
and the only thing I can remember
is the smell of her hair when we used to spoon at night,
her back to me, my face in her hair
and my arms wrapped around her.

INSIDE THE LOCKED HEART

Inside the locked heart
is where I've been all my life
these soft walls around me
beat softly
this red nepenthe flows through me
brings me promises
leaves me waiting for more
always waiting for more.

I don't remember when I started
and I'm sure I won't know it
after I'm gone
but here in this place
this mood
this dream
is where I've been all my life.

And even when I've loved
when these walls swelled with blood
when the fires burned
when I burned
when I could feel the pounding of another heart
inches from me
pressing against these walls
two hearts pulsing as one,
I thought I was finally bursting through,
squeezing out of this muscled prison with raw fingers.
But I wasn't.
I was still alone,
then as now.

Inside the locked heart
is where I'll always be.
until these walls slow their rhythm
and come to a dead stop.

THIS IS HOW MY EVENINGS GO

I approach this table of three women and one man.
I do not know them
but they are part of a wine-tasting group
I joined some years back
and they had a notice on their website
about dinner at this particular bar before going to a
outdoor jazz concert in the park next to the bar.
So I joined them.
As I sit down, the waitress (Katrina)
immediately brings me a glass of wine
and walks away, ignoring the rest of the table.
"How do you get service here?" one women asks.
"The last time we came here, she took forever to bring our food."
"Yes," the man joins in, "the waitress is rude and slow."
"How do you do it?" another woman says, eyeing my wine.
"You just have to have the right touch," I say.
Of course, the right touch is that I tip Katrina 40-50%
every time I go there
which, really, is not that much.
A burger and a beer might come to eleven dollars.
I tip her five dollars.
Big deal. But it pays off.
"Where did she go again?" the man asks, annoyed.
I do not like him.
"Are you all ready to order?" I ask.
"Yes," the women say.
I raise my hand. Katrina appears.
"They want to order," I say, pointing at the women.
She takes their order and then says to me, "the usual?"
"Yes," I say.
Katrina leaves. We all introduce ourselves.
The man, however, does not say anything to me.
That's okay. I do not want to talk with him.

I talk with the women.
One is older, slightly bitter, opinionated.
The second is about the same age, a bit heavy
but rather vapid, silly.
She has large breasts which one assumes
carried the day for her for many years
but not so much now.
The third woman is younger, maybe thirty five,
blondish hair
some rosacea on her face
a bit plump
with a small mouth with small teeth
but not unpleasant looking.
I chat with her for awhile
but soon it is clear, she is not very bright,
unemployed, living with her mom,
looking for a man to save her.

Katrina brings my food first (my usual dish)
then the other people's food.
I decide that maybe I don't want to go
anywhere with these folks
even though it's good to develop connections
with people like these in the event they can introduce
you to their better looking friends, but still...
I do not want to sit with them in the park.
Maybe I will go for a jog instead.

I finish my meal.
"What times does the concert start?" I ask.
"In twenty minutes," one woman says.
"I have to go run an errand," I say,
"but I will try to make it back. Where will you all be sitting?"
They tell me.
"Hope to make it back in time," I say as I stand to go

(with no intention of coming back).
I leave Katrina a 50% tip, as usual, but also to compensate her
for the measly tips I'm sure those bitter and small minded
people will leave her
and I head out of there.
I go home and change into running clothes.
I take the trash out with me on the way out.
But when I open the outdoor trash receptacle
I see a woman's wallet with a driver's license and credit cards
in the receptacle.
I reach in and pull out the driver's license.
I do not recognize the woman.
The wallet has other cards and folded pieces of paper
but no money (of course).
I figure someone stole it, took the money
and tossed the wallet in here.
I sigh, go back upstairs, change back into jeans
and call the police non-emergency line
and tell them what I found.
"We'll send a car over right away to pick it up,"
the dispatcher says.
"Okay," I say, "I'll wait outside by the trash cans."
An hour and a half later, the squad car arrives.
The cop and I exchange pleasantries.
He examines the wallet and the contents and deduces
that it belonged to one of the many homeless that
inhabit this city. Why? Because the driver's license was
suspended and the two credit cards actually were
a food stamp debit card and the type of card that looks like
a credit card but requires a cash balance in order to use it.
He explains that the transients steal mostly from each other,
and the two cards probably had no money on them anyway,
but he thanks me, takes the wallet, and leaves.
It was an educational conversation for me,
but now it is dark and too late to jog

but the bright side is that if I run into those 3 women next week
I will have a real good excuse as to why I couldn't come back
and join them at the outdoor jazz concert
because of my civic duty with the police.
I go back upstairs to my apartment
and pour a glass of wine.

This is how many of my evenings go.
Not really anything to write home about,
kind of a waste of my time
and now
a waste of your time as well.

SPENDING TIME WITH MARY

Spending time with Mary
reminds me of everything that is right
with this world
reminds me of balance
of hope
of love
of loving the moment.

You may not understand this
but there are some people in this world
who remind you that life is good
and Mary
is one of them.
They do not change your world
but they give you a different way of looking at it.

I hope you have a Mary in your life
and if you don't
let me tell you
that you can love the moment
no matter what it is
that there is always hope
that there is always chance
and opportunity
that there is always something to appreciate
that you can be a bit kinder to people that you meet
and that you can take in a bit more kindness from people.

To all the Marys in this world:
Thank you.

WOMEN

I love women.
I love everything about them,
the way they smell
the way they look
the way they sound
the way they plot
the way they twist the knife in
the foolish mistakes they make
to compensate for the worse mistakes
that men make
for example,
I sat next to Sheila in the bar last night
and she was telling me that she always
asks a man on the first date if he's open to marriage
because, she explained, she doesn't want to waste
her time dating someone who isn't open to marriage
because she wants to get married.
I told her that was stupid
(I told her that for two reasons)
I told her it was stupid because men do not know
what they want.
(I said I would never marry
and I did it twice.)
Also, I added, it's the kind of question guaranteed
to scare a man away
when asked on a first date
because it makes them think that the woman
just wants to get married
(which in Sheila's case, of course, is absolutely true).
Then, just to be more argumentative, I told her
that if she couldn't simply intuit
whether a man was open to marriage
by the end of the first date
she had no business dating.

As I say, I told her these things for two reasons,
first, because they are true,
but secondly, and more importantly,
because Sheila is the kind of woman who gets
excited by a good argument.
It's a form of flirtation for her,
sexually stimulating,
a type of early dating foreplay;
because I intuit that she's the kind of woman
who likes a man who can hold his own.

I'm not that kind of man
but I'll pretend to be that kind of man
if that's what it takes
to seduce Sheila.

As I say, I love women.
I love the deceit
the perfume
the banter
the leaning forward
they are just fascinating creatures
until they get old and bitter
which they claim happens
because they hang around
men like me.

ESCARGOT

The only difference between us and snails
is that we can shower off our slime once a day.
We carry our loneliness on our backs
so we have a space to slide into
when the light becomes too bright.
And when our loneliness becomes too small
we find a bigger empty space to carry.

Alice was engaged to someone she didn't love
and broke off with him to fuck some stranger
then the stranger never called her back
and her fiancé wouldn't take her back
so she came crying to me
saying the loneliness was bigger than she could handle,
but eventually she grew into it.
No matter that she didn't love either man.
It's the big empty space we are drawn to more than anything.
It makes us feel at home.

There is no antidote to being a snail.
Well... there is one—it's kindness.
For some reason, being kind to someone
makes them feel human,
makes their shell shrink a bit.
But no one ever does that.
Try it sometime.
Make a resolution to do one kind act
or say one kind thing in a day.
You'll find it's very difficult,
almost impossible.
It's because we're just snails,
and snails are not kind.
And even if you manage through some Herculean effort

to say a kind thing,
you'll find that some people
can't accept it.
Their shells are too thick
and they will slime all over you.

I knew this Ph.D. in philosophy back at the university.
He was a serious student,
studied all the great ancient writers,
actually agonized over the meaning of life,
and when I asked him one time
if he could summarize everything he had learned
in one sentence, he thought for a minute and said:
"I think the best we can do is to try and love others
and try to let them love us."

That was years ago,
but I think he was right.
That's about the best we can do.

The only difference between us and snails
is that we can shower off our slime once a day.

ON KISSING

I feel sorry for the svelte boys at the bathhouse
who like to kiss
because I like to kiss too, but I refuse their kisses
but that's because I don't know them.
(Hookers tell me the same thing:
fucking is not personal, but kissing is.)
If I knew these boys, if we were dating, or living together
I would give them long deep kisses,
thrusting my tongue deep in their mouths
and likewise receiving their tongues
but alas,
I do not know them
so I turn my head when they try to kiss me.
and just let them do those other things to me.

Eve liked to kiss.
She loved to thrust her tongue immediately into my mouth
daring me to suck it hard.

Others were not so bold...
Some, I remember, would just peck at my mouth
with their lips
even when my cock was inside their vaginas
and their legs were on my shoulders.

I have no idea what women think
but I have come to believe that
despite how much they talk with each other,
They don't really compare notes.

GYPSY

The gypsy was sitting on a chair
on the sidewalk
at dusk
by a little table
with a jar
that contained dollar bills.
There was a sign that read
"bibliographic psychic"
and I was walking by.

And as I was walking by
she said, "Do you have a question
for the bibliograph?"
I stopped. "Pardon?" I said.
"A question for the bibliograph.
I am a sensitive, a third eye.
I do readings of past lives."

I looked at her.
Gypsy was the wrong word,
poetic, but wrong.
She was about 40, red hair,
pretty, smiling. I was drawn to her.

And I actually stood there and
thought about it.
What if she was a true psychic?
A true sensitive?

What if you had the chance to ask
someone that one question
that would give you an answer
to something that was plaguing you?

A sense of sadness came over me
and all I could do was smile and say
"I like what you do, but I ran out of questions
a long time ago."

That wasn't quite true
because there's always questions,
but it was the only way I could express it
at that moment.
It would have been more accurate to say
"I stopped caring about the answers
a long time ago."

The questions are still important
and it's important to question
and important to wonder,
but the answers, at least the answers
to my questions,
don't really make any difference,
at least not to me anymore.

When will I die?
Will I ever find true love?
Will I ever find meaningful work?
What is the point of it all?
What should I do?

There's simply no answer
that would make any difference to me.

So I walked on down the block
stopped into a favorite restaurant
and sat at a table by myself.
The waitress knows me well.

I had a bowl of soup
and a glass of wine
and I thought about the gypsy.
I liked her red hair, her friendly face,
her little shawl, her smile.
I was, as I say, drawn to her

I finished my soup and my wine,
paid my bill
and decided to walk back by the gypsy.

I took a dollar bill out of my wallet
and put it in my pocket
thinking that I could sit down
in the chair next to her
place the dollar in the jar
and just ask to look at her face
for sixty seconds
just to draw in that enchantment.

But when I got back to the gypsy,
there was a woman sitting in the chair
next to her.
She had dark hair, also about 40,
and she had put a dollar in the jar
and was saying, "All my life,
I have wanted to...."
as I walked by.

Intimacy is a funny thing.
Complete strangers will open up
to complete strangers
on the spur of the moment.

Separateness is a funny thing too.
It also happens on the spur of the moment.
The connections we have to others
are brief.

I walked past the pretty gypsy
and her pretty client
and headed back to my little apartamento
where I had a date with a real
red gypsy from Spain
named
Rioja Tempranillo.

LIQUIDITY

She was sitting by herself in the Cuttlefish Bar
when I glided in.
I was already fully loaded
and she was electric in the phosphorescent dress
that hugged her like a second skin.
I slid right over next to her,
well, actually,
slightly behind and above her,
and said "I can read your ink, baby,
and it spells my name."
She didn't even give me a look
but I watched her skin glow as I gently
reached around her...

These are the sorts of thoughts I have
sitting in my cubicle
staring at a computer screen
editing some financial document.
The phosphorescent glow of the monitor
seems to pulse
in time with the music
in my earphones...

Those could be the sort of thoughts
she might have
sitting in the Cuttlefish Bar
waiting for Mr. Right to swim on in...

SONOFABITCH

She said something about something
when she left.
I didn't quite catch it
because I wasn't listening.
She always said I didn't listen
and I guess she was right.
It was something about me ignoring her
and her stories about
her mother the mean schoolteacher
her brother the lazy sonofabitch
her daughter the druggie slacker
her ex-husband the manipulative sonofabitch
her father the abusive sonofabitch...
It's no wonder
I didn't listen.
When I hear the word sonofabitch
I generally tune out.
They're all sonofabitches,
I know,
I have no doubt
but they're not sonofabitches to me
because I don't listen to them.

Not listening is an art.
I tried to encourage her
to not listen to them
but my words
fell on deaf ears.

ODE TO ANNYA

To end up like Sal Mineo
or Lucian Carr
or my friend Bob...
He was gay but had married Annya,
an innocent girl from China.
They had a son but then he
stopped having sex with her,
told her he was gay,
but she, being as I say, innocent
and Chinese, stayed married
in order to raise the son.
and he went about his business.

But eventually it got too much for her
and they divorced
but they still maintained appearances
for the sake of the son.

My wife and I used to go to social events
with Bob and Annya and their son.

One night Bob picked up a
young muscular man at the Glory Hole Bar
and took him back to his apartment.
The young man was recently out of prison
and was not gay
but was looking to rob a gay man,
but things went wrong
and the young muscular man made Bob kneel
at the foot of his bed and then
shot him in the back of his head
and then stole his car and tried to flee the state.

He got caught on a gas station surveillance camera
somewhere in Georgia
using Bob's credit card
driving Bob's car.
He was arrested for murder, tried, and convicted.

I was asleep in bed next to my wife
when I got the call
that night
from Annya
the night Bob was murdered.

Annya called me
in anguished tears
telling me what little the police had told her.
Bob was dead,
murdered
found in his underwear
at the foot of his bed
shot in the back of the head.
I knew instantly what must have happened
and I knew that Annya knew too.

I listened, and kept repeating "I'm so sorry,
Oh Annya, I'm so sorry."
What else is there to say at such times?
Afterwards, I told my wife that Bob
had been murdered.
I don't know if she knew that Bob was gay
or that he frequented such sketchy bars
as the Glory Hole,
and I didn't tell her any of that.

I knew about all of that
because Annya had told me over the past few months.

She and I had been lovers,
getting together when my wife was out of town.
She was a great lover,
starved for attention
after years of neglect from Bob
but she felt guilty because she was friends with my wife.
Me? I didn't care.
I was starved for attention too
and I thought the love I brought her
was a way out of my lobotomized existence.

The murder put an end to my affair with Annya.
She thought it was God's punishment for her
betraying my wife.

My wife and I and Annya went to the funeral service
for Bob,
and we sat with Annya all through the court appearances
until things were eventually settled and time passed
and some type of healing started.

I don't know if healing is the right word.
I don't know if anything ever heals.
Maybe it just scabs over.

My wife and I eventually divorced
but by then Annya had remarried
to some nice fellow who helped her raise her son.
I moved west and lost touch with her.

But I know human nature
and I know there must be times
when the memory of
getting that call that night
from the police

about Bob
suddenly comes back to her
the same way that the memory
of the love I tried to bring her
in my own wounded
damaged
mangled
fuck-up
way
comes back to me.

TO YOU, HERBERT

I remember reading *Mind at the End of its Tether*
in college...
It was a book for a class, you see,
and college was a time of drugs, women, classes
and growing up
pretty much in that order...
but I remember reading that book
and the years passed
and the years passed
and now I find
even though I don't remember
anything about the book
that the title alone is enough
to send chills up my spine.

I spend my nights alone
typing out these missives.
I spend my days alone
walking among these misses
and nothing makes any sense
to me anymore.

It used to.
Things used to make sense.

But now, I got nothing.
If I go on a blind date
and the woman asks,
"What do you do?"
I got nothing.
Do I say, "I'm a lawyer working
in a corrupt system that destroys people"?
Or if she asks, "What are your hobbies?"

do I say, "Writing about the horror of
moments like these"?
And God help me if she asks
"What do you enjoy doing?"
because the truthful answer to her would be
"Putting you in handcuffs,
pulling down your pants and licking you
until you screamed in orgasmic fury."
Not the kind of thing a woman wants to hear
on a first date,
certainly not on a blind date.
"I have to leave now," she would say.

I got nothing.
Things used to make sense
back when I was married and was the captain
of our neighborhood watch
and volunteered with the fire department.
Back then I was part of a community.
But now, I am not part of any community,
not with the people in the other cubicles where I work
not with the people in my apartment building
not with the people I meet
not with the people on the street
not with the people in the bars
not with the people in their cars
not with the people I rub shoulders with at the
farmers' market
not with anyone.

Oh Herbert George Wells
I don't remember anything about your book
but your title had it so right.
Damn you.

HEAVEN'S CALL CENTER

In Heaven's call center
there are cubicles stretching into infinity,
each section assigned to certain types of calls.
For example, there's a section for Buddhists
one for Agnostics
one for Taoists
one for Atheists
one for Muslims
one for Baptists, etc., etc.
There's even a section for those who claim they never call
(that section actually gets the most calls).
Some of the sections are cross-trained,
for example,
the Confucianist and Taoist sections
can handle each other's calls
as can the Evangelist and the Muslim sections.
But other sections,
like the Agnostic and the Atheist sections
are strictly forbidden to cross-train.

But the section I want to work in
is the wrong number section.
That's the best section,
because each call is different.
The other sections get so repetitive:
the Atheists always wanting to know why
there's no God
and the Skeptics always wanting to know why
God doesn't know,
the Jesuits always asking about original sin
and the Southern Baptists always wanting
to turn some neighbor in,
but in the wrong number section

you really get the chance to intervene,
to make a difference.

Say for example, someone calls in,
having misdialed the cable company,
wanting to schedule an appointment.
Well, you have the chance to put new thoughts
into their head, like, "Do you really need
247 channels so you can sit on your ass?
Have you looked outside recently and seen
what a magnificent world you live in
where despite all the ugliness, there's luck and
opportunity and people who really want to feel?"

Or suppose someone calls in thinking they're dialing
their girlfriend, or boyfriend,
then you have the chance, depending on how good
the relationship is, to put that thought in their head:
"Hey, maybe this person isn't the one for you,"
or, "Hey, maybe you're missing the fact that this person
is perfect for you, and you should let them know."

Or suppose some old man calls in,
having misdialed the brothel
where he hoped to set up an appointment...
Well now, that's a dilemma.
Should you put any alternative thought
into his brain
or should you just go ahead and
reconnect him to the right number
and let it go?

Oh yes, the wrong number section is a blast.
It's the only place where God lets us be
totally random.

DUCK BLIND

I'm hunkered down
biding my time
in the duck blind,
waiting
for some bird to come into view.
Stuck out in the swamp,
huddled down in some isolated lean-to,
simply waiting.
Although maybe I should call it a fuck blind...
you know, just to make it more apropos
to the situation.

WHY I WRITE

The days conspire against you
methodically
unrelentingly.
You have to work
so you go to work
and although you know that you are lucky to have a job
you still count the hours
every single fucking day
until you can leave,
holding on to the hope of the weekend.
But the weekends are the same horror show,
and the hours drag on there too,
because you connect with nothing and no one.

You walk down by the harbor
and the people that you see—
hideous fat bloated tattooed monstrosities—
seem like cattle to you, nothing more.

You buy a lottery ticket
hoping for a way out.
You think, I will fly away to some paradise
where even if there's no meaning
there's at least satiation and debauchery.
But your numbers never come up
and you are stuck here.

No wonder you drink,
the endless procession of waste…
nothing works,
nothing matters.
You get so damned depressed
but there's nothing you can do

but endure.
Should you go to the bar or drink alone at home?
Should you answer the online ad
that is surely a front for prostitution
or worse, a crazy person,
or should you continue to wait until fate
(if fate exists)
introduces you to someone
who is equally as hungry as you?
Life is a hideous circus.
Everyone is either a carny or a patsy or a rube
and even the patsies and rubes will use you,
given the chance.

And you're repeatedly left with the only choice
that is ever available:
choosing between the lesser
of two agonies.

So you drink alone
and you walk alone
and you stay alone
and you spend your time alone
and you write alone
keeping the only thing alive that can save you—
that tiny flame...
you write.

THE WAY OF SAINT JAMES

The Camino de Santiago stretches in all directions
but all paths end in Santiago
where Saint James is buried.
Life is like that too, you know.
Many paths, all ending in death.

Trace your path along the grooves
of the seashell
where all the grooves
end at the apex,
the hinge that opens
and swallows you.

Does it matter which path you take
if they all end at the same place?
The path through Portugal is wild and pretty
but there are few bathrooms.
This is an important consideration in life.
Therefore I take the French way.
Robert Frost aside,
I prefer the way with more women,
restaurants,
and bathrooms.

Saint James might not approve, I suppose.
But I am walking for me,
not for him.

Some pilgrimages have nothing to do with religion.
Yet I shall walk the Camino de Santiago
and I will touch the pillar of Saint James
in the hopes that my sins will be forgiven
and then I may spend several days in Madrid

lounging in the bathhouses
resting my weary feet
and visiting the brothels
replenishing my weary sins.

LATE SEPTEMBER

Late September,
rain is moving in
and the evenings are getting colder.
I remember you in that thin coat.

Late September,
I've opened a second bottle of wine.

Late September
and I don't want to wonder where you are
because that's what all ex-lovers do—
they wonder where their former lovers are.

So instead, let me send a prayer your way,
let me hope you are wrapped in the arms of a new love,
flesh to flesh, breathless,
wet, enthralled, overcome, satiated.
Why not?
It's the least I can do
remembering the love you brought to me.

Late September,
and the evenings get darker sooner, faster.
It's going to be an early winter
judging by the moss that grows
on my heart.

THE LONG ROAD

Over hill
over dale
as we hit
the dusty trail
and those caissons keep rolling along...

When I was a child, I had a 78 rpm record player
and these phonographs of children's songs
that were really military songs.
Who would give a kid such garbage?

When I was a child, I played in the woods,
talked to the snakes and turtles,
wondered at the fireflies
and the sound of the bullfrogs.
Who took away my native tongue?

When I was a child, I was in love
with a girl in the fourth grade who sat
three seats behind me.
Nothing mattered but her.
I would have done anything for her.
I would have died for her.
Who took away my commitment to love?

And now, 60 years later,
all I want to do is speak in my native tongue
and fall into that kind of love again.

But you know what they say about first times...
they once happen once.

THE JUDGE

I sit here
in my black robes
listening to the expert witness
testify
as to the psychological qualities of deviants
and I place a silent checkmark
on each quality that applies to me.
Anti-authority? Check.
Obsessed with sex? Check.
Impulsive? Check.
Deceitful? Check.
Manipulative? Check.
Ambiguous sexuality? Check.
Prefers prostitutes? Check.
Unable to form lasting relationships? Check.
Loner? Check.
I don't get them all, mind you.
After all, I have some restraint,
but once again I find myself
staring at a defendant
and thinking:

there but for fortune....

EVERY NIGHT

I dream the camino every night.
I walk, or fly, or sail, or fall
but ever I dream.
I always dream of moving from one space to another
moving without moving
yet taking step after step
the weight on my back
holding me
to the earth
like the weight of my life,
my loves, my memories,
anchoring me to this life.
Without this weight of memory,
I would float away.

I dream the camino every night.
Faces appear for an instant
but then are gone.

And in the day, it is exactly the same.
Faces appear for an instant
but then are gone.
The day makes as much sense as a dream.
It is a dream.

I dream the camino every night.
I must walk.
I'm afraid also
that I must die.
I dream the camino every night.

Maybe death will simply be
taking off the backpack
and the boots,
laying down the walking sticks,
and just floating away.

DURABLE POWER OF ATTORNEY

Everyone wants to die at home
but few do.
By the time death comes knocking
someone else is making those decisions for you.
And it's more profitable for your doctor
to keep you hooked up to those machines
in some steel cold room
than to let you die at home.

The doctors,
the hospitals,
the insurance companies,
all want a say in your last hours on earth.

And the mental powers of stealth
that once would have allowed you
to easily slip their clutches,
well, those powers are gone.
And there you are,
frail, blue lipped, out of breath,
thoughts slipping away like
wisps of smoke.

And those who you once could trust to come to your aid
are gone
or worse,
want you tucked away somewhere too.

Not much to look forward to.

Better live wild while you can

before the legal documents kick in.

SOMETHING

I want to believe that something
is in the process of being born,
that these nights on the gallows
and these days on the wheel
are but spiritual contractions
from which something new
will spring forth,
something that will somehow
make sense out of everything
that went before.

That's the great logical fallacy, you know,
that we use the things that come later
to make sense out of what happened before,
as if winning the lottery
somehow justified the years of grinding poverty.
"All those years of eating beans were worth it
because without them, I never would have won."
As if the years of suffering bought the winning ticket.

It's total insanity,
but still, I want to believe that something
is in the process of being born,
that something deep in the shadows is
forming, gaining strength, getting organized,
about to emerge into my consciousness,
a new clarity, a plan, something
that will make sense
out of this mess
that I call
my life.

Sense for a while, at least,
before death steals everything away.

CLEANING UP

I was cleaning up the bedroom
doing laundry, vacuuming, picking up shit,
decided to rearrange the books on my bookshelf,
and saw the book of Shakespeare's Love Sonnets
that she gave me
back when our flame burned so white hot bright.
I opened it to read that sweet inscription she wrote
when she gave it to me

"My dearest love,
'Kind in my love today, tomorrow kind,
 still constant in wondrous excellence'
             from Sonnett CV
You are my heart, my soul, my love."

Of course, she left me 6 months ago,
which reminded me of a few other Shakespeare lines,
especially the one about frailty.

But I put the book back in the bookshelf
and continued cleaning.
I can move on too, you know.

LAMENTATIONS

The lawyer's lament:
    stuck in meetings all day
    chairs as hard as church pews
    fudging the billable hours
    fudging my promises
    fudging my dreams

the whore's lament:
    it never feels good
    no matter what they think
    it never feels good

the preacher's lament:
    I learned the technique
    the proper delivery
    the rise and fall of intonation
    they listen and nod their heads amen
    when I preach,
    but I don't believe the words
    anymore

the divorcée's lament:
    it all slipped through my fingers
    and all the men
    are just as flat and boring
    as he was

the fortune teller's lament:
    the worst part is
    I never get to find out if I am right
    I make my best prognosis
    and never see them again

the wine merchant's lament:
    they opened a big self-serve wine discount store
    across town
    I can't compete with their prices
    all my "loyal" customers have disappeared
    I gave them all my knowledge
    but all they want is price

the artist's lament:
    I thought I had arrived
    when the gallery agreed to show my paintings
    but day after day
    nothing sells

the doctor's lament:
    I know Avalide would work best
    but insurance will only pay for Chlorthalidone
    so I prescribe Chlorthlidone
    and keep my mouth shut

the masseuse's lament:
    why bring relief
    to the tension and abuse
    they inflict on themselves?
    aren't I just enabling them
    to continue their abuse?
    I should increase their pain
    not diminish it

the soldier's lament:
    I just don't want to die here
    so I accept that I'm willing to kill
    and I embrace the doctrine
    and I repeat the doctrine
    although all I see are villages

       straight out of the middle ages
       I just don't want to die here

the dealer's lament:
       15 dollars an hour, plus tips
       that's what I'm paid at this table
       while the yahoos come in and lose
       thousands
       my job is not to roll my eyes
       when they bet the hardways

the cab driver's lament:
       in my country
       I was a doctor
       but I fled during the war
       and have no proof of my schooling
       so my skilled hands grip the wheel
       instead of the surgeon's tools

my lament:
       the dreams I had as a youth
       will not materialize
       I look like everyone else
       none of my effort will amount to much
       and no one will care
       what happens to me

THE INVISIBLE MAN

You don't need to take a potion
to become invisible.
Trust me.
It's not science fiction.
You don't need a potion
or another dimension
or a fantastic wavelength transformational machine
to make you invisible.
You don't need a magic spell
or a magic cloak
or creatures from outer space bearing gifts
to make you invisible.
You just need time.
Just a little time.
Let yourself grey a little.
Trust me.
You'll be invisible.
No one will see you.
You'll be able to walk down any street
without making even a shadow.
People you know will not even see you.
Trust me on this.
It's easy to do.

PEOPLE I KNOW

There's this woman I know...
She's divorced.
She spends her weekends schlepping
her teenage kids to various events...
I don't do that.

I know this guy,
married, he's remodeling his kitchen
at his wife's request,
spends all weekend sanding or painting or repairing
comes to work exhausted every Monday...
I don't do that.

I know this other guy,
active outdoors type,
spends every weekend with hiking groups or rock climbing,
he's always off exercising somewhere...
I don't do that.

I know this other woman...
She's always traveling,
every weekend.
She's off to this festival or that event
hundreds of miles away.
Sometimes she disappears for months
out of state, out of country...
I don't do that.

I know this other guy,
rarely leaves his apartment
and if he does, he only walks downtown
and drinks alone at a bar
and doesn't talk to anyone

walks the street and looks at people
as if they were from some other planet...
I do that.

WHEN ERNESTO GOT OUT OF PRISON

When Ernesto got out of prison
I helped him find an apartment.
He didn't like the first three we looked at.
They had tiny windows.
He'd take one look and walk out
saying, "It reminds me of my cell."
Finally we found one with a balcony
and big sliding glass windows.
The view of the city was ugly
but it was a view.
"I like it," he said, "I can see out."

When Ernesto got out of prison
he couldn't find a job
because of his convictions.
Finally he learned to start every letter
with: "I just got out of prison
and I need a job. Let me tell you why
I would be your best worker."
Finally he got a job as a proofreader
working the night shift.
It didn't pay much, but he liked it.

When Ernesto got out of prison
all his old friends started coming around
wanting to talk about the good old days.
"Go away," he told them. "I work nights.
I need to sleep during the day."
Besides, hanging around with them meant
he'd be violating the terms of his release.

When Ernesto got out of prison
he didn't last too long.

One of terms of his parole was no alcohol
and one morning he got home after a long night's work
and had just cracked a beer
when his parole officer made a surprise visit.
They revoked him for eight months.
He wrote and asked me
if I would help him find another apartment
when he got released.
I wrote back, "Of course."

I understand how hard it is.

We're all under conditions of release
And we're all constantly getting violated.

STREET LIFE

Sonic was stabbed under the bridge. They stuffed his body into a barrel and tried to burn it, but bodies don't really burn that well. The police eventually arrested Skitzo and his buddies Red and Discord. Joker heard the news as she was getting out of rehab. She knew Sonic and kinda liked him. She was mad at Skitzo. But it's a family out here on the street. And you just don't turn your back on your family, no matter what they do. Joker just shook her head and walked off to the food bank.

SALES CONFERENCE

It was one of those nights
that had a force all its own.
I touched her hand at dinner
and didn't let go
and she didn't move her hand away.
Later, we went back to her hotel room
and without words, started kissing,
took off our clothes and went to bed.
The next morning she caught a plane
back to Chicago
and her husband.

I saw them three months later
at another sales conference
and she and I acted as if nothing had happened.

In fact, the acting was so good
I began to wonder if it really had happened.

DON'T LOOK NOW

The guy at the end of the bar
hasn't been with a woman in six months,
has given up the chase,
no longer goes to the dances, the meet-ups,
no longer hits the happy-hours,
no longer looks at the personal ads on Craigslist.
The guy at the end of the bar
has found his own personal nirvana
or personal hell
depending on how you look at it.
He drinks quietly, maybe makes a little conversation
with the bartender, but that's about it.
He barely looks up if a woman walks in.
He's thrown in the towel,
taking the ten count,
bought the farm,
has hung it up,
taking the dirt nap
taking the long way
home.
The guy at the end of the bar
used to be the envy of his married friends
living it up, loving 'em and leaving 'em,
the swinging life
the single life
but you know how it is,
age has a way of catching up with you,
and with the guy at the end of the bar.
You know how it is,
how it all ends up,
don't you?

IT CHANGES THROUGHOUT THE DAY

In the morning I actually like her.
She lets me enjoy my coffee quietly,
lets me reminisce about the day before,
about the day ahead.
She leaves me alone for the first few hours
of the day
and I get a lot of work done,
but after lunch she begins to ask questions,
small ones at first
but they grow more unnerving as evening
approaches.
Dinner is usually quiet
but after dinner is hell.
The rattling of pots and pans
The oppressiveness of being trapped
in that small apartment with her.
I have to get out
and go somewhere, anywhere
to be away from her.
Sometimes I make it out the door
but I always return home
empty handed,
and she always welcomes me,
saying, "See, I knew you'd come back to me.
I'm the only one who knows you."
And it's true.
I open a bottle of wine
and sit down to talk with her,
my true love,
mi corazón,
my faithful companion:
Solitude.

TRAIN WRECKS

The saddest thing is watching train wrecks.
They happen to everyone.
You watch them happen to your friends,
or to total strangers.
The guy about to get fired at work,
the neighbor talking about his sure-fire investment,
the defendant taking a bad plea deal....

And then there was you tonight
after the cops said you were okay
and left
after I talked with you for awhile and realized
you were not okay.
"Does she have any weapons?" the cops asked me
when they arrived. "No," I said.
"Is there any alcohol or drugs involved?"
"No," I said, leaving out the part "not tonight anyway."
They talked with you and I stood off a ways
but I watched you put on that "everything is okay" act
and explain how we all just misunderstood,
although it's a little hard to misunderstand the email
you sent out saying: "I'm going to kill myself now."

The saddest thing is watching train wrecks
yet sometimes there's a certain pattern.
Take you, for example,
young, stunningly beautiful, bright, quick-witted,
fun to be with, excessively consumptive,
the life of the party, the center of attention,
yet always unhappy
your path littered with men,
drama, and bad choices.
They should have named you Marilyn.

RALPH WHITEWAY DIDN'T LIKE HIS NAME

So he changed it to something exotic:
Rafael Via de Blanco
which is Spanish for
Ralph Whiteway.
And even though he had red hair
and pale skin, he thought it sounded better
when he introduced himself to girls
at the bars
as Rafael,
although everyone knew he was Ralph.
It was a small town.

He eventually married a girl named Pam,
a quiet girl, who never talked,
but she worked hard and saved up her money
for her one big dream.
And when she had saved up enough money,
she bought her dream.
Came home one day with brand new tits.
She was very proud of them
and they were stupendous,
especially on such a thin girl.
She was so proud of them she showed them to everyone,
and soon thereafter divorced Ralph.

I don't know what people do with the little time we have
here.
I don't know what we're supposed to do,
but I suppose we all want to shed our skin like snakes,
metamorphosize ourselves like butterflies,
change our namesakes and our bodies
and fly away.

I know I would
if I could.

MEMORIES ARE MADE OF THIS

"I remember when you used to
bring me a beer every Thursday night,
and you took me out to dinner occasionally,
and there was that one time you took me
to the hot tubs
and I kept thinking, 'doesn't he know
he'll never get into my pants?'"

"Ha," I said.

"Then we drove down to Brian's that one time
and you tried to kiss me in the pool,
and I said, "It'll never work out.""

"I remember," I said.

"And remember when we were at that bar
and you wanted to dance and I didn't want to
because I was afraid people would think
I was dancing with my dad?"

"Yeah," I said.

"Yeah," she said.

"Listen," I said, "would you like to go out for breakfast
or should I just make you something here?"

"Let's go out," she said.

"Okay," I said, and I got out of bed and started looking
for my underwear.

WHAT WOMEN WANT

Even Freud didn't know
(and he had all the answers)
so there's no point in someone like me
even trying to understand.

Men, of course, want a certain predictability.
Women, on the other hand, seem to want a certain progression.
These are two quite different things
which often leads to problems.

If I go a long time without women
I sort of forget how they feel,
how they taste,
how they smell
but when I'm with them
I can't get enough.

Ali sits up in the bed
but I push her back down
and push her legs apart and go down.
She says, "No, I haven't showered,"
but she tastes great and soon she moans
softly while my tongue nibbles, probes,
dives in and out, drinking her sweet juices.

I don't think Freud went down on women much,
if ever.

If he did
he still wouldn't know what they want
but he might know what they like.

WHEN YOU GONNA WAKE UP?

Ever been in a dream where you can't stop
the bad feeling?
Say you're driving a truck at night
and the headlights are out
and there's no streetlights
and you hear the voices of children
by the side of the road
but you can't see them
and you're speeding because
you're supposed to be somewhere
but you're lost
and the gear shift is too far to reach
and the brake pedal keeps slipping
and don't have a license
and you're afraid the police will stop you...
and you want to change everything:
you want the headlights to work
you want to know where you're going and why
you want to just stop the truck and get out
but you can't....
When you wake, you lie in bed and think about it.
It was a bad dream that you had no control over.
It leaves you with a crappy feeling, wondering
what it meant.

You start thinking about people:
the ex-wife whose life continues like a train wreck
whom you worry will end up a suicide or homeless,
the ex-girlfriend who could never stop talking about herself,
beautiful, anorexic, who is quickly abandoned by every man
she meets, including you...
the ex-boss who drove the knife into the business
causing everyone, including you, to quit.

And you think about all the things you said to them
to try and get them to stop what they were doing,
all to no avail.

All the people you know speeding like a broken truck
without headlights or brakes
lost in life.

Some people are just like a bad dream
you can't fix them
you just have to walk away.

STAND-OFF

We were lying in bed when I said
"If we get married, promise me you'll stop shaving down there."
"Why?" she said.
"I like a lot of hair."
"Do you think we would get married?" she asked.
(She's 35, I'm 62)
"Sure," I said, "someday when you're not in your right mind."
"Ha," she said, "why don't we then?"
"Huh?"
"We could get married. Let's do it."
I sat up and looked at her.
"Will you stop shaving down there?"
"No."
"Then we can't do it," I said, lying back down
feeling a bit relieved.

MOON

We don't feel the moon
but it pulls the tides and the menstrual blood.

We feel the heat of the sun
but not its weight that spins us round and round.

The physicist says there's no gravity without mass
yet now my flesh aches for you
and you're not here.

We take gravity for granted.
We take everything for granted.

DINNER

This is how I know I'm growing older:
I enjoy the act of taking a woman out to dinner.
It's a beautiful ritual,
a beautiful thing unto itself.
Younger men see the dinner as the price they pay
(literally) to get the woman to bed.
But to me, whether the woman wants to go to bed
with me or not, well, that's up to her.
I don't push it.
But I do enjoy the dinner, especially if I know the place
and they bring me wine before dinner
then a small Caesar salad
and all the while I am talking with some marvelous creature
about how her day went, her plans, her problems.
And then there's the main course,
and we talk about that
and I try her food, and she tries mine.
It's a beautiful thing,
but all beautiful things come to an end.
So I'm on the phone with Mary tonight
complaining how Ali is down in San Diego
and Catalina is moving to Kentucky
and I don't have anyone to take out to dinner,
and she laughs
and says "Roberto, if the past is any indication
of the future, there will be a lull, but then, lo and behold,
some creature will come into your life to fill the void
and you will have your dinners again."
She's right, of course,
although sometimes the lull can last for many months.
Still it's good to have something to look forward to,
and I'm looking forward to taking someone out to dinner,
maybe you.

GIVE UP

The waiting time between lovers
is something all lovers endure
but don't talk about.
When one affair ends
and the feelings scab over a bit
you start thinking ahead
(we all do it, so don't say you don't)
because you know that eventually
some new creature will arrive
to either sweep you away
or fuck you up
but either way there will be (hopefully)
some glorious boundary violations
in the bedroom.

You've been around the block
so you know how it is—
eventually a new lover arrives.
The problem is the waiting time.
You have to wait.
Nothing you do can make him or her appear
any faster.
No amount of internet dating or barroom sitting
makes Fate hurry her damn ass sweet time.
In fact, *trying* to make it happen just makes it take longer.
You just have to wait.
The problem is that the older you get,
the longer the waiting time.
It can take months, maybe even a year
before a new lover comes into your life.

That's why God invented bathhouses.

THE BATHHOUSE

You pay your $20
and the attendant hands you a room key and a towel
and says "Have a good time"
and buzzes the door open
and you step inside
and walk up dark corridors
and you find your room
and step out of your clothes,
wrap the towel around you
head for the showers
and then into the steam room
where it is dark
and steamy
and you can't see anyone's face
but that's the point
and as you move slowly around the steam room
some hands find your ass
and some hands find your cock
and your hand finds someone else's cock
and there's a dance and changing of partners
and after enough dancing and titilation
eventually some mouth finds your cock
and you cum.
After resting a bit, you shower off,
head back to your room,
back into your clothes,
and eventually out the exit door
into the blear of sunlight,
the city streets and
heterosexual world
that has no idea of what you do
why you do it
why you need to do it

and why you will do it again next weekend
and every weekend thereafter
until someone real comes into your life.

IN THE REALM OF INFINITE POSSIBILITIES

She called me up to tell me
about her newest love
how they kissed for the first time
then how on the next night they made out
then how on the next night they lay down
in her bed and made out for hours
but because she didn't have any condoms
they didn't take their clothes off and have sex.
(She explained that it had been so long
since she had had sex with a man that
she had thrown away her shoebox with condoms and lube.)
She really likes him, and he treats her respectfully.

Sounds good, I said.

She says that they have a date
for this coming Wednesday.
(I bet both of them manage to accidentally
buy some condoms by then.)

I'm happy for you, I said.

And I meant that sincerely because the fact is,
he's a better match for her. He's 31, she's 29.
I'm 62... You see the problem.
So I'll bide my time and be a good listener
because, who knows, in the realm of infinite possibilities,
he could mistreat her,
they could split up
and she may need a shoulder to cry on,
and I'm a good listener,
and I always keep a box of fresh condoms
by the bed.

WHAT GOD WILL NOT FORGIVE

I think I must have been about 15 years old
when I saw the movie Zorba the Greek
and Anthony Quinn said to Alan Bates,
"God is merciful, but there is one sin he will not forgive—
when a woman calls a man to her bed and he will not go."

As I said, I was 15
and it made a big impression on me.
But that was more than 45 years ago
and many things that make an impression on a 15 year old,
one learns as one grows older, are total crap
(like authority, rules, logic, or justice)
but those two lines, I have found,
have withstood the test of time.
Now I don't know if those lines are true or not,
I only know
that I have lived my life
trying to follow them
as if they were true.
"God is merciful, but there is one sin he will not forgive—
when a woman calls a man to her bed and he will not go."

Everyone needs words to live by.

HOW ABOUT YOU?

It's raining outside.
Is it raining where you are?
I've opened a second bottle of wine.
Are you drinking?

I wrote all day.
What did you do?
Then I wandered down to a bar
but there was nothing for me there
(there never is anymore)
so I walked home still sober,
but I'm working on that now
while the rain pours down.

I like the rain
because it doesn't give a damn what anyone wants.
It just rains.
I hope it rains all night.
It makes it pleasant to sleep.
And I hope it rains tomorrow,
because I plan to drive to the big city
where there is a certain bathhouse,
and when it rains, more men come to the bathhouse
looking for something to do.
What do you do when you're looking for
something to do?

I had breakfast today with a beautiful woman
who told me how she picked up a fellow at a bar
the night before
who ate her out
and made her come.
That's nice.

I could have saved her the trip to the bar, but hey,
it's her life.
Maybe she likes a challenge.
Maybe I'm too easy.
I don't push it anymore.

My glass is empty.
I don't feel that old but evidently I am.

I wonder what you are doing tonight.
I spent a quick moment perusing the online ads
this evening,
you know, the things that purport to be dating services.
It's such a turn-off.
It's amazing anyone actually mates.

When it comes to relationships,
nothing really works,
at least not for me.
How about you?

When I think of past good relationships
all I ever remember is certain sex scenes.
Is that true for you?
Or do you remember something else perhaps,
some act of kindness from the other person,
a certain look in their eye?
I confess, I remember those things too.

I'd like to think we have something in common,
you and I,

but I know
I am mistaken.

FACEBOOK

I found her on Facebook.
I didn't think it had been
that many years
but evidently it had.

I remember that time in Wisconsin.
She was wearing a yellow sundress.
It was strapless.
She was sitting in the shade
of a large tree
and smiling at me
because she loved me.
The light dappled on her bare shoulders.

It's funny how some images remain frozen
in your brain
forever.

But that was another state
another time
and evidently
another world.

I found her on Facebook.
I thought about friending her
but when I counted the years
I decided not to.

I hate that people age,
that we thicken and become hard.

I found her on Facebook
and then I let her go

again.

TIM

My friend Tim was a musician.
He used to drive a cab in Chicago
because, you know, music doesn't pay the bills.
Tim, like a lot of musicians, was also a philosopher,
liked to read Nietzsche, Alan Watts, etc.,
liked to talk philosophy with his passengers.
One day he picked up an older fat cat from
the Mercantile Exchange and they got to talking
about the meaning of life.
The fat cat was smoking a big cigar
(it was back in the day when
you could smoke in cabs)
and he said to Tim,
"What do you think the secret of life is?"
and Tim rattled on about meaning
and personal growth,
and the fat cat said, "Bullshit,"
and blew smoke from his cigar,
and said,
"The secret of life is gold and sex."
That pretty much ended the conversation.

Except that I think the fat cat was wrong.
Gold is not the secret of life.

But sex is.

CATALINA IS A BURNING TATTOO

She wanted to cover this tattoo
on her left arm.
I wasn't sure exactly how it would be done
but she found an artist in Portland
who did magic with the needle and ink
and now the Garden of Eden blooms
on her arm
and leaves and flowers envelop her body.

The intimacy of the tattoo artist is total.
You surrender your body to him (or her).
You bare your flesh.
You submit.
You wince in pain
as the needle injects color under your skin
and there is nothing you can do but submit
while he takes his time,
leaves his mark
on your body.

I could never be a tattoo artist.
As much as I want that kind of intimacy
I could never do it.
I never want to leave my mark
on a lover's body
anymore.

Love leaves its own tattoo
and the invisible scars on the heart
can't be covered up by new lovers
no matter how artistic they are.

MISS AMANDA

Miss Amanda was a Clairvoyant
so they said,
a Sensitive, a Psychic, a reader of Palms,
and a reader of the soul
so they said
and so I went
one balmy evening
when the wind blew the leaves down the street.

I liked her immediately,
her smile, her twinkling eyes.
I placed my twenty dollars in the small box
on the table that sat between us,
as my friends had instructed me to do.
And I held up my palms
as she instructed me to do
and she looked at them for a while
without talking.
Finally she said, "What do you want to know?"
and I said, "Tell me about relationships,"
but of course what I meant was
"Tell me about my love life."
I was too shy to ask that directly, but I could tell
she knew what I meant.
She looked at my hands a bit more,
turned them, studied the sides of them,
and finally said,
"You will have lovers but no true love.
You see these many small lines here,
these are all relationships, some very pleasing
but no long lines, no lasting lines,
no permanent enduring relationships.
Many lovers, no love."

Later as I walked home through the blowing leaves
I thought to myself, I didn't need to spend $20
to find that out. I already knew that.

But that's why we go to fortune-tellers, isn't it?
Because that's what we all yearn for,
that long love, that deep love, that enduring love,
that special someone, that true love.

We spend all our lives waiting for it
hoping for it
preparing for it
planning for it
primping for it,
buying for it
shaping up for it
slimming down for it,
adjusting for it
searching for it
hoping for it.

And we see it in the eyes of everyone we date
or are introduced to
or meet at the party
or the bar...
that brief microsecond tell in their eyes,
that says "Are you the one?"

Well, I guess I have confirmation now.
I can honestly answer,
"No."

FARMERS MARKET

I walked down to the farmers market today.
I didn't need anything,
just wanted to get out.
There were people all milling about
examining the displays of
lettuce, carrots, potatoes,
rutabaga, breads, fresh pastries,
asparagus, radishes, tomatoes,
peppers, apples, pears,
peaches, emu cream, lavender sprays,
quilts, t-shirts, smoked salmon
beef jerky, chicken jerky, turkey jerky...
There were stands selling tacos,
noodles, salads, hummus, bratwursts,
sandwiches, coffee, sodas,
and corn dogs for the kids.
There were picnic tables crowded
with people eating and listening to
live music from a small stage.
People were walking all around
talking to each other
going from stand to stand
enjoying the day.

I walked down to the farmers market today.

I just don't fit in anywhere.

GOD'S WILL

I suppose if there is Divine Intervention
there must be Divine Interference,
you know, when God puts the mic too near
the speaker,
when he cranks up the gain,
creating that feedback and distortion,
puts that annoying hum
in the soundtrack of your life,
just enough to throw
your timing off.

I was walking down by the pier
and came up on three fat ladies each walking
their tiny dogs.
They were walking three abreast
taking up the entire width of the wooden pier
oblivious to the fact that I had walked up
behind them
and I said "Excuse me, ladies" as I squeezed by
and they each gave me the dirtiest look.

Is there any noise reduction in heaven?
Or do the angels just drink wine
like we do?

The woman had her driver's side door open
and the man was standing beside the open door,
leaning in to talk with her,
and I could hear her say as I walked by,
"You've gone back to her, that's your choice,
but don't come crying to me when she screws it up.
You and I are over."

And I walked on, thinking, okay, she got to the point,
maybe that needed to be said,
but when I was walking back, about an hour later,
they were still there, still talking.
Evidently she and he were not over.

Jesus said there was no marriage in heaven,
so evidently they are smarter than us up there.

I was sound asleep, taking an afternoon nap
when there was a knock on the door.
I got up, opened it, and there
were these two eighteen-year-old girls,
both quite pretty,
each holding a packet of pamphlets.
"We're here to share the good news
that God has forgiven your sins," the first one said.
I looked at her, hoping that she was at least eighteen,
wondering if there was any way in God's green earth
I could get her into my bed.
"I don't believe that there is any such thing as sin," I said.
This took them back a bit.
"The Bible says there is sin," the second one said.
"I don't believe in the Bible," I said.
The first one sputtered a bit and then replayed the tape
that had been programmed into her head.
"We're here to tell you how your sins can be forgiven."
"As I said, there is no such thing as sin," I repeated
but then I decided to give them a break.
"But you might want to try the guy on the first floor,
in the first apartment. He's a Satanist, and he believes
in sin. In fact, he advocates for it. Maybe you can help him.
Now, unless you two want to have a drink with me,
I'm going back to my nap."

Needless to say, they did not want to have a drink with me
and I went back to my nap.

If there is some great plan
I'd like to know where I fit in.

Sometimes the noise drops off
and things just happen.
Like when I ran into the waitress
from my favorite bar at the grocery store
and she gave me a big hug
and she gave me her email
and said she'd like to go out with me.
That was a distortion-free event.

But then the mysterious hand of God
reached over and turned up the
Divine Interference
and her email replies to me
made no sense and were full of
misspellings,
and we never went out.

There was the time of the Great Flood
and the time of the Great Plague
and there was that Great War (or two).
Maybe this is the time of the Great Distortion,
the Great Distraction
the Great Interference.

Or maybe, as Tom Waits once said,
there's no Devil,
there's just God when he's drunk.

WE LIVE OUR LIVES AS METAPHORS

Here is the girl with the slow cancer
who says that life matters.
Here is the old soldier
who says that life is pointless.
Here is the young unemployed hipster
in the coffee shop who says life is jive...
We categorize everyone we see
into a box
into a metaphor
into a shorthand short story with a
shortstop ending.
Look around you,
the bespectacled student
the beleaguered clerk
the shiftless bum
the unctuous funeral director
the pious preacher
the prim librarian
the polished speaker
the pontificating politician
the smiling salesman
the cheating spouse
the unappreciated cubicle worker
the heartless IRS man
the corrupt judge
the flirting barmaid
the smooth player
the inept technician
the good husband
the good wife
the preacher's child
the juvenile delinquent
the tomboy

the overworked nurse
the ignored wife
the MILF next door
the prostitute with the heart of gold
the gold digger
the petty thief
the rock star
the aging rock star
the has been
the
the
the
we put a label on everyone,
and each of them live the label,
they act out the metaphor
exactly the same way
as we do ourselves
following the script
line by line.

Which one are you?

Worse... which one am I?

ALI-CAT

She was feral,
that's the only word for it.
We'd be driving somewhere
and she'd suddenly get horny,
unzip her jeans
reach down
and start rubbing herself,
demanding I reach down there too
(which I did, while driving).

I remember one day
she called me at work.
I rushed home
just as she arrived.
We had our clothes off
as soon as I locked the door
and we went at it
without speaking.

Odd thing was,
you could never give her
a compliment.
She'd bristle if you did.
She only wanted to fuck,
and then she'd let you feed her
at some restaurant somewhere.

She was feral
and now she's gone
like that cat that used to come around
and then one day
just disappears.

NOTHING IS FREE

She told me how it went down:
how it was a hot July day
and she was inside her apartment
sweating but horny
wearing a t-shirt with no bra
thinking about masturbating
and how her neighbor came to the door
and she answered the door
in her t-shirt and no bra
and he made some nice comment
(after all, he had been pursuing her
for months)
and because it was a hot July day
and because she was horny,
she thought, "Well, why not?"
so they did.

But of course, everything has
unintended consequences.
For her, it was just an afternoon fuck
but for him, it was a dream come true.
He thought she was finally acknowledging
that he was the one for her
and so, a few months later
when she started fucking me
on a regular basis,
his heart was broken
and he blamed me
and he blamed her.

It was like a story my friend Brett told me:
He was at an outdoor concert years ago
walking in the woods away from the crowd

and some girl walked up to him
under the trees
obviously stoned out of her mind
and said "Do you wanna fuck?"
and so they did
right there on the trail.
He never got her name.
And he thought afterwards
"Well, that was marvelous,
so free, easy, and natural."
But about 3 days later
his dick started to hurt
and there was this nasty discharge.

Back in the 8th century BC,
the Greek poet Hesiod said,
"Before the gates of excellence
the high gods have placed sweat."
I don't think he was talking about sex,
but maybe he was.

BANKING PROBLEMS

I go to my bank to make a deposit.
That was easy enough.
I hand the girl the check, and
she hands me a receipt.
But then I ask, "Do you have
any Sacagawea dollar coins?"
and she looks at her coin tray.
"No," she says, "all I have are these,"
and she holds out a handful of
Sacagawea dollar coins.
"Those are Sacagawea coins," I tell her.
"How many do you have?"
She looks at them and counts.
I see her lips moving.
"Eight," she says.
"I'll take them," I say, handing her eight dollar bills.
She looks at the image on the coins
as she hands them to me.
"Who is she?" she asks,
and I explain that she was the Native American guide
who helped Lewis and Clark explore America.
I could tell she didn't know
who Lewis and Clark were either,
but she smiled nicely.
But as I leave I wonder how a person can
work at a bank and not know about money.

Later that night, I am trying to set up
online banking with Bank of America
which they claim is easy to do,
but there's some glitch
and I keep getting an error message.
So I call their 24-hour customer service line,

and the lady on the other end says
it's not me, there's a glitch in the system,
and she transfer me to a "specialist" whom
she says can help me, and I then talk
to Leo, their "specialist", who asks me
what time it is where I am.
And then he has me try a few things, and then
he says there is a glitch in the system and I
should try again in two days.
"Two days?" I ask him.
"Yes, in two days," he says.
"That's a pretty big glitch," I say.
"Yes," he says, "try again in two days."
Now I'm wondering how you can have a world-wide
money/investment/banking system as large as
Bank of America, and have a glitch that takes
two days to fix.

I can't get my head around that,
so I revert to my common everyday explanation
for such problems:
People are just fucked up stupid everywhere.

HARSH

I read a phrase in a personal ad
where it says "describe yourself"
and the woman wrote
"shedding like a cheese grinder"
and this confused me:
because I could not tell if the writer
was trying to be cute,
ironic,
whimsical,
or was merely stupid...
but of course,
there I was
reading the personal ad
which is a rather hideous thing
when you think of it
(the fact that I am reading it, not
the fact that she wrote it)...

How would I respond to such an ad
from a 34 year old
writing about shedding like cheese
when I, at 62, am molting like a bird
or a crab—
becoming what?
A 62 year old man perusing personal ads?

It's a shame really,
because much of her "profile"
is rather funny
and if someone sitting next to me at a bar
would say such funny things,
I would respond
with some witty repartee
because I'm not without resources,

yet
this is online dating
which has different rules
and one of the rules is that
62 year old men
do not respond
to
34 year old women
who
shed
like
cheese
or
who
might
not
even
exist.

It's harsh I know,
believe me, I know.

There is simply no way
through the magic of the internet
(even if I say something witty
that she connects to)
that when she asks my age,
she will not recoil
in horror.
She may give it another name
other than "horror"
but the outcome is the same.

So I move on,
to look at other ads,

saddened
but illuminated
in the glow
of the
computer
monitor.

AGUIRRE AND YOU AND ME

There's this movie I saw once,
Aguirre the Wrath of God,
about this fierce leader of men,
Spanish Conquistador,
sailing down the Amazon
looking for gold
who, in actuality, is mad,
but so belligerent in his leadership
that none oppose him
but follow obediently
and all die one by one
from native arrows, or disease, or starvation,
until Aguirre is left alone
sailing what remains of his ship,
now only a raft,
barking orders at the monkeys
and rats
who are his only companions.

Most organizations are like that, you know.
Full of madmen, or madwomen.
and usually there's one seemingly normal person,
like First Mate Starbuck in Moby Dick,
who convinces the others that everything's okay
and yes, he knows the captain is mad, but hey,
we've been through this before
and we can do it again, he tells the crew,
and they listen from their oars,
or, in the case of most organizations,
from their cubicles...
And everything does continue
until the day some disaster hits.

Disaster doesn't always hit, of course,
but when it does, it comes with a vengeance
as the Enrons crumble
and the HealthSouth executives are indicted
and the Tycos are gutted
and the Bear Stearnses fail
and the Lehman Brothers collapse
as the AIGs are exposed
and the BP oil tanks explode
and the WorldCom executives go to jail...

Yes, disaster comes with a vengeance
when it comes...
but it doesn't always come;
and some of the time
(in fact, most of the time)
the madmen
or madwomen
simply get away with it.
They get promoted up and
out of the way,
or ease into retirement,
and the monkeys on the raft
and the rats on the raft
and the workers in their cubicles
drift on
down the Amazon,
and the First Mate Starbucks
are promoted to managers
due to their loyalty,
and corporate life goes on,
because, my children,
that's how business is done.

OVERHEARD

I was walking in my favorite park.
The sun was out.
It was a beautiful day,
not too hot, not too humid.
A group of women were walking towards me.
They were all talking about something.

And as I passed them, I heard one say to another,
"There are still plenty of guys out there worth dating."
And when I heard this,
I took a quick look at them,
especially the one getting the advice.
They were attractive women,
in their thirties,
and the one getting the advice was nodding
in agreement
as if to say, "yes, there must be guys out there
worth dating."
Of course, they didn't even see me,
didn't even look my way
not even a glance
as they walked past me
while I was looking at them.

They say that women have this radar,
that they can size up a guy
from any distance,
from across the bar,
or across the park,
but I thought maybe their radar
was fucked up.
I wanted to stop and say
"Hey, I'm a guy worth dating"
but of course I didn't,
because the thought also occurred to me
that maybe I'm not.

I DIDN'T KNOW

I didn't know it was possible
to feel this lonely.
I come home from my dinner
with Catalina,
a dinner with no connection,
two people at a table,
talking, but no connection.
I walk home
passing the empty bars
where I usually drink,
passing the couples arm in arm on the sidewalk,
seeing the young girl with her man at the motel check-in,
noticing the number of older men
like me
walking alone.

Catalina told me she was invited
to two barbecues this weekend,
plus she's going kayaking with some guy,
plus she's met this other guy
that she's interested in,
plus she having breakfast with a friend on Sunday.
She asks what I'm doing this weekend.
I don't answer,
because I know what I'll be doing this weekend.
I talk to no one.
I see no one.
I have no plans,
except maybe
on Sunday
if I'm still alive
I'll go to the bathhouse
and let some stranger blow me,
just to have some type of human contact.

WHO DO WE THINK WE ARE?

Catalina and I were walking in the plaza
in the bright afternoon
under the shade of the mango trees
under the watch of the old Catholic iglesia
and she was telling me how she has vowed
to stop staying up all night
because she owes it to her little students
not to show up all sleep-deprived
at the school where she teaches,
and how she is going to stop drinking so much
because she woke up puking last weekend
after staying up until 2 or 3 in the morning
drinking with her friends
at the local bar.
"It's a good plan," I told her, and we sat by the fountain
and discussed meeting for dinner that evening.

Much later that night I said my goodbyes.
It was midnight and I needed to get some sleep.
We had gone from the restaurant to a bar,
and then to another bar where there was music.
She was on her fourth or fifth margarita
dancing with her friends
having a great time
making plans to go with them to yet another bar
and dance the night away,
and after all, it was a Saturday night,
and Catalina is young, and her friends are fun,
and they all like to dance.

At any rate, I gave her a hug goodbye,
told her I would call her the next day,
and made my way home.

There is such a disconnect between our intention
and our actions.
No matter how much we plan,
we humans simply cannot change

The next day I did call her
and she was very hung-over
so we postponed our plans
for church.
And she swore to me again
she was going to stop partying so late
on Saturday nights.
"That's a good plan," I said,
and we discussed meeting later in the week
at the plaza or maybe for lunch somewhere.

Catalina's no different than you or me.
We cannot change.
We might have change thrust upon us
by events
such as losing our job
getting a DUI
getting older
etc.
And then maybe we adapt a bit
because we have no money
or there's no bar in the jail
or our liver gives out,
but the idea of us deciding to be different
and then, through a force of pure will,
being different…
why, it's an illusion of pure lunacy,
the ultimate egocentric megalomania.
Who do we think we are?
Even the gods can't change
by simply making themselves promises.

THE GAME OF LOVE

I have my own personal theory about sports.
I think that sports were solely invented to give us metaphors
and to be specific, that they were only invented
to give us metaphors about relationships.
For example, when you strike out on a date,
or maybe you get to third base
before you chip out on the final hole.
Or you're in the bar at closing time
and you've been swinging and missing all night
and you're down to your last strike
and the clock is running out
and you just need that one knockout punchline
so you try one last Hail Mary pass
but it comes out of left field,
misses the goal,
and she turns away
and you're out of the game.

Not that sports metaphors make any more sense
out of relationships than gambling metaphors,
hunting metaphors, astrology, psychology,
advice columns,
or self-help books.
It's just that sports metaphors are funnier
because they're more stupid.
People actually believe you get three tries
at getting a hit in the game of love...

There's nothing more stupid than a sports metaphor.
And nothing dulls the ache of loneliness
like good old stupidity.

OCCUPATIONAL HAZARD

When she asked me what I did
I told her I was a writer.
"Ooooh," she said.
"Show me some of your writing."
So I handed her a notebook full of poems,
and she thumbed through them.
"These are depressing," she said.
"Yes, I know," I said, and refilled her wine glass
and changed the subject.

That is usually the problem with younger women.
They haven't seen enough death,
so life is one big promise ring to them,
and the older ones who've had their eyes opened,
well, they don't want to be reminded.

I put the notebook back on the shelf,
put some music on,
and made a promise to myself
that the next time a woman asks me what I do,
I will tell her I'm a plumber.

WAITING ROOMS

There's always a waiting room:
in the hospitals, in the lawyer's office,
at the airport, at the dentist,
at the funeral home,
always a waiting room
where you wait
alone with your thoughts.
And no matter where it is
my thoughts are always the same:
I think about death,
and about the impending pain
I am about to face,
(from the doctor, dentist, lawyer,
preacher, or mortician)
and I think about the breasts
of young women,
the different sizes, the different
nipples, the different tastes...
Or if not the breasts,
then the other parts
which are just as good,
if not better.

After all,
you have to think of something
to get your mind off the
real reason you are waiting.

HUNGER

I watch the long-legged blonde
walk past my table.
She does not look at me.
That's okay, I understand how it is
between men and women.
She will look at me when she wants to,
when she is looking for a man.

All the men in all the bars around the world
try and chat them up, make them laugh,
buy them drinks,
and all the men in all the bars around the world
don't understand why they go home alone
when they were having such a *good* time,
and when they do get lucky
they think it was because
they were witty or charming
or because they are handsome.
But I know how it is.

When you are not hungry
you will walk past 100 restaurants
no matter how appealing they are,
no matter how well they advertise themselves,
but when you are starved,
you will stop at the first joint that is open
as long as it isn't a total dive.

So I sit and wait.
Eventually someone will walk by
who is hungry.
I have a good location:
I'm just over the hill
and easy to get to.
I'm not a total dive
and I'm open for business.

THE REGULATION OF PEE

A. Piaget said that the regulation of pee was the first step in the socialization of the child; learning when to pee, how to pee, and most importantly, how to hold back from peeing.

B. I see a young mother in the park with her little boy. She is holding him by the shoulders against the wall that surrounds a church. He is peeing on the wall. Evidently he needed to go, and she is directing him how to pee on the wall.

C. When I was a child, the funniest poems were signed by I. P. Freely.

D. Vonnegut said humans were invented by water as a means of transporting itself around.

E. I am older now and get up several times a night to pee.

F. My last girlfriend and I peed on each other in the shower. I am 62. She was 35. Then we got out of the shower, dried ourselves off, and went and had a wonderful fuck.

G. I drink lots of water at night, and lots of coffee during the day.

H. I think the world is crazy. Maybe the socialization process is not going so well. Maybe if we all just peed freely, the world would be a better place.

STARING AT THE WALL

I remember listening to R. D. Laing explain
how these parents had called him
complaining that their teenage daughter
must be schizophrenic because she just
sat and stared at nothing for hours.
They wanted to have her committed.

He went to their house and met with the girl
and determined that she was not schizophrenic.
She just liked staring at nothing for hours.
So he taught her to cross her legs
and face the wall,
and he explained to her parents
that she was just meditating.

I could sit and stare at the ocean all day
but I'm an old man so no one pays me any mind.

I write pornographic stories
but I publish them under an assumed name.

I go to gay bathhouses whenever I travel
but never in my home town.

I have this one girlfriend who really likes rough sex.
I keep the windows closed whenever she comes over.

Sometimes the difference between being crazy
and being sane
is not getting caught.

NEW ORLEANS

I remember waking up one morning
in New Orleans
where I had been helping an ex-lover
(who happened to be lesbian—
but that's another story)
get out of an abusive lesbian relationship
(the butch beat her).
I got to play the heavy—the bodyguard—
while she moved her stuff out.
But that's another story too.
Anyway, the point is,
I woke up in bed with my ex-lover
and we both were hungry
and she said, "I know this great little place
for breakfast."
So we got up, got dressed
and walked down the street.
There was a line outside the place.
There was also a dead body
lying there on the sidewalk.
A sheet was thrown over it
but the sheet had shifted somewhat.
His face was still covered
but the rest of him was exposed
and he was clearly dead.
As the line moved forward, each person
stepped over the dead body.
My ex-lover and I ended up
behind the two policemen who were
investigating the dead body.
They too were hungry
and had decided to get something to eat
while they filled out their reports.

"Do you think he jumped?" the first cop asked.
"Yeah, it looks like it," the second one replied.
"I'll mark it as a suicide, then," the first one said.
"Sounds good to me," the second one replied.
A waitress showed the two cops
to their table
and another waitress showed me
and my ex-lover to our table.

I have two takeaways
from that memory.
First, I remember that my lesbian ex-lover
had the biggest clit of any woman
I've ever slept with.
I used to love to suck on it
as if it was a small dick.
Unfortunately, she was primarily a lesbian
so I only got to do that when
she was in a rare mood for a man.
Secondly, whenever someone tells me
horror stories about murders and crime
in Panama (where I now live)
I think back to that time
when the line to the popular restaurant
in New Orleans
proceeded along in order,
each person in turn stepping over
a dead man
who was lying in the street.

WHEN THE MUSE SAYS GOODBYE

I don't know why so many great writers
take their own lives.
Ernest Hemingway
Richard Brautigan
Hunter Thompson
Violeta Parra
Hart Crane
and hundreds more.
I just don't get it.

Right before Phil Ochs killed himself
he said, "The words just won't come anymore."
Maybe that's it.
Maybe writers who only find life meaningful
when they create meaning
through their words,
can't go on without their words.

Hemingway left one of his best works—
Islands in the Stream—unfinished
when he killed himself,
and now when you read it
you feel the unbearable weight of true loneliness.
The part where Thomas Hudson sails
across the ocean
to attend the funeral of his wife and 2 sons
will send shivers up your spine.

I don't know why so many great writers
take their own lives
but I take a bit of comfort in the fact
that there are enough deficiencies in my own writing
that I'll never be placed
in their category.

ANT TOWN

We're as mad as ants
building our little worlds
completely oblivious to the forces
that will kick our hills to dust.

Order is everything in Ant Town
and order is good
and order works
and progress is made
until the dust-kicker comes.

If you live in Ant Town
everything makes sense.
If you live in the U.S.
everything makes sense.
In any culture, the culture makes sense.
Stone you to death for adultery?
Of course.
forty years in a cage because you possess
a drug that makes you stupid?
Of course.
No contraception?
Of course.
Everyone in Ant Town knows the rules.
Everyone in Ant Town understands.

The true difficulty in escaping Ant Town
is that you have to leave the other ants.
And that means you have to live alone.

That's the problem with freedom.
You have to do it by yourself

and you have to be
alone
for a long time,
a very long time.

WHAT SAPPHO SAID TO APHRODITE

To be born female
is to be made crazy.
You soon learn that your purpose
is to let a man inject you with seed
so that you will incubate babies.
You will be given dolls
to practice with.
You will be given rituals
to explain it all.
You will be indoctrinated.

You will look at your body
and see the slit where the
seed is injected
and the teats to feed the child.
You will examine your body
for evidence of any other purpose,
but there is nothing else there.

And when you are young
the men will line up
and they will cajole you
and you will lie down
and open up
and they will stick themselves into your body
to deposit their sticky semen.

To be born female
is to be made crazy,
is to be given such an emptiness
such a loneliness
and then to be told
that only a man

and only a child
can fill that emptiness.

And for a while
you will accept that.
You will say yes to every man,
and you will say to them
fuck me, fuck me now, fuck me harder
fill my empty hole, my empty soul,
cover my womb with semen,
fuck my cunt, my mouth, my ass—
let me be connected!

And if you are foolish
or unlucky,
you will get pregnant,
and the cycle of slavery
will begin again.

To be born female
is to be made crazy.
And nothing can stop
the craziness of it all.

You ask me why I only sleep
with women?
I ask you why you don't.

THEY THOUGHT THEY WERE FREE

It was a time when the local police
were being heavily militarized,
marching around in new uniforms
and new weapons.
Racism was endemic in the language,
and de facto segregation was everywhere,
although nobody used that term for it,
but hate crimes were clearly increasing,
although the state called them
civil forfeitures.
And the legislators kept passing
new laws
restricting where people could go,
what they could do,
and most importantly,
what could be taught in school.
Voting district lines were redrawn
and strict identification papers were
required,
to keep the poor from voting.
The main newspapers were all
propaganda,
and any dissenters were quickly
marginalized.
Real estate prices soared,
and the gap between the rich
and the poor grew worse.
Even making rent became
impossible.
The bureaucrats blamed the homeless
for being poor
and left the problem to the police to solve.
The churches remained silent

or joined the right wing
and grew prosperous.
All limits on buying politicians
were removed,
and eventually
the banks and insurance companies
controlled every aspect of business
and every politician.
But the most prosperous industry of all,
hidden under a million different names
so that its magnitude was totally invisible,
was the war industry.
Business was good
and the stock market soared
while the homeless and the disenfranchised
and the masses of expendable workers
suffered, fell ill, and eventually died,
somewhere out of sight.

And the weirdest thing of all
was that it all felt normal.

It was Germany, 1939.

Welcome home.

SAY WHAT YOU WANT

Say what you want about the homeless,
but it's tough out there on the street.
You can whine about how they get
free food and free shelter
but when you live on the street,
you have NO SENSE OF HOME,
and no sense of stability in your life.

Say what you want about the homeless,
how uneducated, stupid, and crass they are,
how they stand around and beg for coins,
but when you're out on the street,
you have NOTHING TO DO,
and no sense of meaning in your life.

Say what you want about the homeless,
about how they chose to live this way,
how they chose to drop out of school
how they chose not to have a career,
but remember, no one moves to the street
because their previous life was better.
No one moves to the street to give up a place
where they were loved and cared for,
and most of all, protected.
When you're out on the street it means
NO ONE LOVED YOU where you were before.

Say what you want about the homeless,
how they live off the system
at the expense of good tax-paying citizens
who live in nice homes and work for a living,
how they add to the crime rate,
cheapen the downtown area,

and are a burden to society,
but remember this,
YOU CREATED THEM.
Yes, you created them...
When you refused to put sex education
in the schools,
you created them,
when you refused to provide free contraception,
you created them,
when you refused to support abortion on demand,
you created them,
each and every one.

You can say what you want about the homeless...
but please don't.

EVER NOTICE

Ever notice how nobody really wants
you to succeed?

Once upon a time I worked in this small office
and one day I bought a sandwich for lunch
at the Safeway, and on a whim,
I also bought a $20 lottery ticket,
and I took my lunch back to my office,
and while eating my sandwich,
I scratched off the $20 lottery ticket
and I had won $100.
I was so surprised I took my ticket next door
to my best friend's office
—my best friend—
and I held up the ticket and said,
"Rick, I just won $100"
and without missing a beat, he said:
"Fuck you."

That's how people are.

Once upon another time I worked in a city
and I had decided to move to another city
a thousand miles away
because I thought (correctly it turns out)
that I would be happier there.
And a good friend of mine did everything
he could to talk me out of it.
"Oh, it rains all the time there.
"You won't be happy there.
"You'll never find work there," etc.
I didn't listen to him and I moved anyway
and I never heard from him again.

That's how people are.
They really don't want you to do
what you want
because that means you will leave them.

And what that means
is that if you ever
want to truly change your life,
you will be doing it alone
totally by yourself
because no one will help you
because they don't want you to change.

I tell you this so that you will understand
that the feeling of being totally isolated
always accompanies people who
try and change their lives.

Of course, it also accompanies people
who do insane things

which is another reason why
most people don't change.

ALI SAID TO ME ONE TIME IN BED

We were lying there just talking
about some friend of hers
who had just gotten married,
and I asked her
"Why did she marry him?"
because I had met the dude
and I was not impressed.
"Well, at the time," Ali responded,
"it was her best option."

That says a lot, I thought to myself,
that choosing a mate comes down to
your best option at the time,
but, like an idiot, I pressed the issue.
"Her best option for what?" I asked.
"You know, for a good life," Ali said.

"Then, how is she not a whore?" I asked.

"Well, people gotta do
what they gotta do," Ali explained,
and looked at me and smiled.

ATTENTION SPAN

First it was the 30 minute
TV show,
then the 2½ minute MTV
music video,
now it's the 40 character
tweet.
Our attention span is being crammed
into smaller and smaller
pinpoints of awareness.
So now it's all instant conclusion,
immediate reaction
to everything in the world,
when what everything in the world
really needs
is the slow reaction,
the considered analysis,
the reflectful thought.
You think I'm mistaken?
Look at you.
You're bored after a 20 line poem.

CRAPS

I admit it.
I play craps occasionally
at the casino.
But I am a wrong better.
I only bet with the house
against the other players.
I play the Don't Pass line
and the Don't Come line
and I always lay the odds.
I don't win much
but I never lose
because I know that in craps
as in life
the dreaded 7 comes up
way too fast
and steals everyone's dreams.
So I bet on it happening,
and while the dealer is raking
everyone else's chips
off the table,
he's paying me.
That's how life is, my friend.
You're going to crap out.
And while it's lonely
being the only wrong player
at the table,
enduring the glares and hatred
of everyone around you,
if you count on everything fucking up,
at the end of the long evening
you'll be the only one left standing.

THE THING ABOUT ALI

The thing about Ali
that you have to understand,
is that it's all about Ali:
her problems, her drama, her needs,
and her sexuality.
But that's what draws you in,
isn't it?... her sexuality...
because it's certainly not
her problems, her drama, or her needs.
It's those rare occasions
when she takes off her clothes
and stands there
with that exquisite body
and lets you run your tongue
anywhere and everywhere
over that exquisite body
and then even she gets excited
and forgets all about
her problems and her drama
and lets her need for you take over...
That's what keeps you coming back,
isn't it?
Even though you know
how it will end:
one day, down the road,
when her naked body
is not quite so exquisite
and her problems and her drama
outweigh any need
she might have for you,
and outweigh any thing
she can do for you...
Then it will end,

and then, years from now,
you will say, "the thing about Ali
was that it was all about Ali"
and years from now
she will say
the same about you.
And you'll both
be right.

CONDENSATION

I think of you
and one image immediately
fills my mind.
We were standing on a bridge
on a bright cold Northwest Pacific day.
You had a red scarf wrapped
around your head
to keep your ears warm.
You were smiling.
You were always happy.
I can feel my face soften
as I look at you...
You seem to be smiling right at me.
There's this shining in your eyes,
I can almost touch your face...
and then you fade.

I write your name on the bar
in wet letters
from the condensation
that has formed
on the bottle.

DE MINIMIS

When you're in the spotlight,
one misstep and you die the death
of a million Twitter cuts
and a million civil suits.
You lose your job, you can't go out in public,
and you are scorned, shunned, and ridiculed.

But I think there must be
a karmic law of de minimis
that says that the Fates
will not fuck with you
if you stay under the radar.

It's the mob that actually
carries out the work of the Fates.
They like nothing better than to
take down their icons,
find some fatal flaw in the heroes
they once glorified,
and to use it to beat them to death.
And there's no shortage
of flawed protagonists.
Macbeth, Lear, Icarus,
Elliot Spitzer, Lance Armstrong...

But hubris is common.
Tragedy requires more than hubris,
it also requires a spotlight.
You need to be on someone's radar.

But I'm safe
and you're safe
because no one knows me
and no one knows you.

So let's keep it that way, okay?

THE BARREL

I never liked the old man.
He always had an opinion
about everything.
He could talk at length,
and he did
especially about himself.

But when the doctors told him
that the lymphoma had returned
and there was nothing they could do,
and he only had a short time left
and that time would not be pleasant,
the old man was quiet,
and then he said,
"well, I guess it's my time in the barrel"
and not another word.

That's when he earned my respect.

IT'S A COMMON STORY

"I don't think about sex," she confessed
sometime around our third date.
"I mean, it can be alright but...
I never really want it. I'll do it
if I really like the guy and he insists."
She was an attractive woman,
late thirties, maybe early forties.
I asked her about her marriage.
"Well, he said he didn't need it either,
so it was a good marriage,
until I found out he was gay
and spent all his free time
at the gay bathhouses.
So we got divorced."

I wasn't surprised.
It's a common story, actually.
Our dinner arrived and we
talked about other things.
I knew she liked me
and had this been ten years ago
I would have insisted
because I did want to fuck her
but tonight it seemed like
too much trouble,
so after I took her home,
I headed over to the bathhouse.

THE SIMPLE LIFE

I am relaxing in the hot jacuzzi.
I am naked.
The water bubbles about my balls.
The jacuzzi is big enough to hold
about ten people
but I am the only one here
because it's only about one in the afternoon
and most customers don't start arriving
until about two o'clock.
I got here early because I wanted to just
relax in the jacuzzi by myself
without any temptations
and let the jets massage my lower back
which is sore from yesterday's workout.
Next to the jacuzzi is a swimming pool.
It is empty.
The steam room is also empty
but full of glorious steam.
By three o'clock the jacuzzi will be full
of handsome naked men
and the dark corners of the steam room
will be full of handsome naked men
having sex with each other.

The gay bathhouse.
There's nothing else quite like it.
What a marvelous place.
What a glorious place.
You can let yourself feel totally natural,
totally without shame,
just celebrating your own nakedness,
your own maleness,
your own sexiness.

Just remember to always use a condom
and don't let anyone cum in your mouth.

PACHINKO

You make your bet,
the ball drops
and you hope the fates
will be kind.
But life's choices are limited.
There's a finite number of bounces
from post to post
until the ball stops.

The house edge is unbeatable.
The best bet is not to play,
just walk away.

I know, I know...
You can't resist the advertising,
the music and the crowds.
Marry this girl and you'll be happy.
Buy this house—the mortgage is easy.
Get this degree and you'll be successful.
Take this job and your future
will be paved with gold.

And I agree—they are great prizes,
but it's all a con game
and you *will* lose.
You will lose all that you love.

I understand... there is no other casino.
Life is the only game in town,
and I know the glitter and the music
and the free drinks are so enticing.
I'm just telling you how it is.
You *will* lose all that you love.

The best bet, the only bet,
is not to play.

POETRY IN ACTION

Catalina writes me and says,
"I want to write a poem that explains
why it is that every man
looks for his next conquest
and every woman wants to be seen
as though she is the only woman
in the world."

And I write back and say,
"If you could answer that question,
you'd be a Goddess."

And then I think,
no poem could ever say it better
than the way she just said it.

Why does every man
looks for his next conquest
and every woman wants to be seen
as though she is the only woman
in the world?

I try to call her back to tell her
that she's already written the
perfect poem,
but she tells me she's about to go
out on a date,
and will call me back later.

STUCK

The beach cottage's sale price
was too good of an offer to ignore,
so Eddie bought it
because his wife convinced him
they needed a place to go to relax
on the weekend because his job
was so stressful.
It is a nice place.
They go every weekend.
But now he's stuck with 2 mortgages
and can't quit the stressful job he hates.

Eddie's been married for 28 years.
I've met his wife.
She's high maintenance.
He's still paying off
that new kitchen she wanted.
It's a very nice kitchen.
The contractor made them a good offer
for the remodeling.
Eddie married his wife because
he was so in love.
Love always seems like a good offer,
but now his life consists of bitching
about his wife, or bitching about his
life, working at a job he hates, and
paying off 2 mortgages and the kitchen.

His wife was working for the state
when they met.
It was a dead-end job
filing treatment reports
but then they offered to pay

for her Master's Degree
if she'd sign a contract to work
for them for 3 more years.
It was a good offer, so she took it.
Afterwards they promoted her
to Child Protective Services
and gave her an impossible caseload
counseling raped children.
She couldn't quit because of the contract.
She did the 3 years but hated the work.
It turned her bitter.
She just wanted out.
She married Eddie because he loved her
and it seemed like a good offer,
but now she stands in her new kitchen
and wonders where her life went.

I don't get around much
but the few people I do know
seem horribly stuck in life,
and the weird thing about being stuck
is that every problem
was the solution
to a previous problem.

IN SOME MOVIE I SAW YEARS AGO

This old hooker is banging on the front door
of this fleabag hotel,
demanding a room.
With her is a nervous john
who doesn't want to be spotted
patronizing a prostitute
(you know how that is).
The night manager shuffles to the door
and the john is getting more nervous,
and while the hooker is arguing
with the manager about the room price,
the john panics and slips away.
Finally the room price deal is struck,
but when the old hooker looks around,
the trick is gone,
and the hooker blames the night manager
because he was so slow
and the night manager feels bad
because this hooker is so old and wrinkled
that she probably doesn't do much business,
so the night manager offers to pay her
what the john was going to pay,
to compensate her for her loss,
and the old hooker pauses,
looks the night manager up and down,
then says, "I don't do it for the money,
I do it because I like it,"
and smiles in a way
that sends cracks across her face
and gives him
the come-hither look.

Now it's the night manager's turn
to panic.

LAYS

The makers of potato chips have discovered
that there is just the right combination of
salt, spice, sugar, and snap
that makes potato chips irresistible.
You may regret it in the morning
but right now they taste just great.

They've invested years of research
and they are still trying to tweak the formula.

But women discovered this long ago
and got the formula down pat.

Bet you can't eat just one.

TEMPUS FUGIT

I have to be honest with myself:
I'm getting old.

I look in the mirror each morning
and see the wear and tear of time.
No hairstyle or skin cream can
hide what everyone sees
when I approach a building
and someone opens the door
for me.

I console myself with the fact
that there are still the bathhouses
and prostitutes.
They will always be there
no matter how old and decrepit
I might become
as long as I can navigate
the steam rooms without a cane,
and as long as I have money.

But I have to be honest with myself:
I'm as young as I'm ever going to be.
From here on forward
It only gets worse.

I don't want to have to stop every
two blocks and rest
in order to catch my breath.
I want to pound the girls hard
on the mattress.
I want to hear the young men moan
and lose control.

I don't need to be young,
but I don't want to be old.

THE LIST

The deterioration one sees
in the world
is just a mirror
of the deterioration
one sees in oneself.

Except in this case,
it's 8 in the morning
and I'm looking in the mirror.

The man in the mirror
is mouthing something
by Beckett.
I can't go on.
You must go on.

So I do what I've always done:
pour a cup of coffee
and make a list
of things to do
and the order in which
to do them.
-run
-call Giselle about Spanish lessons
-buy more 3x5 cards
-write Catalina
-pay bills
-plan trip to Sámara

I feel better,
so I start breakfast.

Nothing like a to-do list
to keep you off suicide watch.

WHEEL OF FORTUNE

"Have you seen my face?" is what Jean-Paul Sartre
is reputed to have said to Albert Camus
when Camus asked him why he tried
so hard with women.

It's true, the wheel of fortune
gives us each a face.
Some handsome, some not so much.
I've seen mine.
It's not so much.

A pretty face is like a free pass
to an adult Disney World.
All your drinks are free
and you can ride any ride you want
as often as you want.
But faces like mine, well...
there's an entrance fee.
It's usually around $40
at Maxine's,
and the rides are pretty short.

But that's how life is.
You get the face you get.
If it's not so much, you'd better
have some money.

But all rides come to an end
and here's the weird thing:
Albert Camus was a handsome man,
Jean-Paul was not,
yet they both came to the same conclusion:
that life was a meaningless
pile of horseshit.

But I still think Camus got more sex.

INVITATIONS

It's Thanksgiving evening
or Christmas eve
or your birthday
and you're drinking alone
not because there weren't invitations
but you don't do invitations.
You never have understood why
you are this way
but you've been this way
all your life.

You remember the first time
you realized you had this twisted
non-participation.
You were about 6 or 7
and your mother offered to take
you and your brothers to the zoo,
but you said no
even though you wanted to go,
and she said, are you sure?
and you were adamant,
so she took your brothers to the zoo
and you stayed home
in your room and cried
because you really did want to go
and you didn't understand why
you told her no.

Well, fast forward 5 or 6 decades
and you're still doing the same thing.
No matter the invitation
you always say no
even though you want to go.

And if they ask why not,
you respond with the usual reason
that you don't like groups
or you're just not feeling social,
but of course, that's not it at all.

And so you skip the Thanksgiving dinners
the wine tastings, the parties,
the Christmas dinners,
the housewarmings,
the birthday parties.

We are all programmed,
wired up to be who we are
long before we know
who we are.

You think it's different for you?
It's not.

Look, here comes your mother
through the door
asking you if you want to go to the zoo.
Let's see what happens
this time.

THE TROUBLE WITH STORIES

I was having lunch with Catalina
and I started telling her about this
bio-energeticist that I used to know.
It was going to be a funny story,
but Catalina asked me
"what's a bio... what you said?"
and I explained how bio-energetics was
a therapy derived from Wilhelm Reich's
Orgone Theory,
and then she asked me
what that was,
and who Wilhelm Reich was,
and so I explained,
and she said "Never heard of him,"
and then our food arrived,
and we got talking about food we liked,
and then later, over dessert, she asked,
"What was that funny story
you were going to tell me?"
and I said, "Oh, never mind,
it wasn't that funny."

When young people say that old people
never have anything to say,
there's a reason.

XEN

Bodhisattvas who impart zen
have a tough gig: to teach you
to be totally responsible
and at the same time,
not to try.

I can't do either.

If I could just modify the doctrine a bit,
if I could teach xen instead of zen....
Xen, the doctrine where you take
a little responsibility, maybe half,
but at the same time,
don't give a shit.

I think people would really get
behind this,
for a small fee, of course.
I've already got the first 5 books outlined:
Xen, the Middle Class Way
The Xen Trust Fund
Monetizing Xen: Let it Be Green
The Prenuptial Xen Contract
Retiring the Xen Way...

Buddhism is referred to as
the Middle Way, the reconciliation
of extremes and the regulation of
one's impulses through ongoing effort.

I teach the Lesser Way,
letting yourself flow to your
lowest level,

like water finding its own depth,
the Easy Seepage we call it
in xen,
the giving in to all desires
within one's budget.

I think there's a market for this.
I think I've got a winner.

WHAT HAPPENED TO US?

Happiness ruins a lot of relationships.
Remember, back in the day, how we
would get together and commiserate
on why we couldn't find someone to love?
We did that for almost two decades.
We were there for each other,
for the lonely years,
the desperate years,
the late night phone call years,
and the I-need-some-advice years.
I always said that you saved my life.
What happened to us?
Well, you found someone to love
and for that I'm happy,
and I enjoy your updates on Facebook,
and I am happy for your new job
and I love the pictures of your new house
in the suburbs and the new puppy
and the vacations with your husband,
but I miss my friend.
All the updates
and the xmas cards
and birthday cards
and the occasional phone call
just aren't enough.

Some people believe
that all relationships have an
expiration tag.
I don't want to believe that,
but I know that change happens
whether we like it or not,
but I still feel the same...
and maybe that's the problem.
You moved on
and I didn't.

UNDER MY SKIN

I cut my foot when I stumbled on the stairs
and jammed my flip-flop foot into
the sharp stone edge of the step,
creating a ragged-edge wound under
my big toe.
It was a stupid misstep.

I was climbing up the long stairway
coming up from the outdoor jacuzzi
at the beautiful gay hotel
where I was staying
in this beautiful beach town.
I was distracted by something,
maybe my years.
It was a long climb
and the day was hot.

I tried to wash the wound the best I could
at a faucet by the swimming pool
sitting with my back towards the naked men
frolicking in the pool
so they wouldn't see the results
of my clumsy perambulation,
or the blood.
Blood is something you don't want to see
around a gay hotel.

I couldn't go into the pool after that.
I lay on a lounge chair under an umbrella
with my toe bandaged,
drinking piña coladas, and watching
the naked men frolic in the water.
"I cut my foot" I would say when they asked
me to join them.

I stayed at the beautiful hotel
for two more days before returning
to my not so beautiful apartamento
which is not located near a beach
and where there is no pool
and where no naked men frolic.

I try to look at the bright side
of most things, but this was just
a stupid accident that fucked up
a nice vacation.

I won't be able to go back to
that beautiful gay hotel
until next year,
but I will go back,
and next year I will bring sandals that
cover the toes,
because next year
I want to be in that group
of naked men frolicking in the pool.
It's something to look forward to,
and we all need something
to look forward to, don't we?

In the meantime I will amuse myself
with the bathhouses and with whomever
might come into my life, male or female,
and of course I will always be careful
to use condoms and practice safe sex
because we all know how important it is
to watch your step.

THE CIRCLE OF LIGHT

Gurdjieff once said that
consciousness is like
walking in the dark
with a flashlight.
All we know is what we see
in that small circle of light.
As soon as something disappears
from the light,
we can't remember it at all.

And then there's that old story
from India, about the four blind men
each describing the elephant…

But you really don't need metaphors
about consciousness to know how
limited we are.

Just talk to the next person you meet

or better yet,
read something you recently wrote,
like for example,
this.

REAL LIFE

Nothing I write compares to real life,
like Sheila telling me about a conference
that she's going to in Tucson,
and how three friends (two guys and a girl)
wanted her to carpool with them,
but she turned them down because
she had slept with both of the guys
and had introduced the girl
to an ex-lover that the girl was now fucking.
Sheila turned down the free ride
because she thought it would be awkward
riding for five hours in a car
with two people she had fucked
and a third who was being fucked
by a guy she had fucked.

You can't make shit like that up.

KILLING TIME

Actually, it's time that does the killing.
It kills you slowly
by eating you alive,
bite by bite,
and when time is done with you,
there's nothing of you left,
not even a memory.

I'm sitting in some park
in the shade
doing nothing.
Somewhere a chained dog is whimpering.

Catalina emailed me last night
telling me her friend Beth had died
the day before,
exactly three months after
Beth's husband of 25 years had died.
Now neither one of them exist.
They're not in a better place—
They simply do not exist anymore.

And one day Catalina will not exist,
and I will not exist,
and you will not exist,
and at some point after that
no one who knew us will exist,
and then,
all memory of us will be gone.

Nothing that we are or have done
will exist.

Buddha said it
more than 2000 years ago:
"You *will* lose all that you love."

PERFECT BREASTS

"I have perfect breasts," she announced
one time when we were in bed.
It was either before or after sex,
I don't remember which, but she thrust
them out for me to admire.
"Aren't they just perfect?" she asked,
and before I could answer, she added,
"I just love them—they're perfect, and
they're just the right size too. Look at them."

It must have been after sex, because
I don't remember saying much,
except to agree with her.
They were nice, but the fact was,
they were just breasts,
nice enough, pretty enough, but
that was it.
And although I didn't tell her,
I actually prefer smaller breasts,
but mostly I prefer
more interesting conversation.

THAT THIN WHITE LINE

I saw a falling star tonight,
a quick thin white line
that zipped across the cold black deep.
If I had blinked, I would have missed it.

when I asked the palm reader
if I would live a long time
she looked at me and said:
who knows?

you would think a falling star
would screech across the sky,
traveling thousands of miles per hour,
burning white hot,
but it was total silence.

maybe when you're traveling
thousands of miles an hour
in empty space,
it's like not moving at all,
and you never see the atmosphere
before you hit it
because it's invisible.

it's only when you hit air,
that BAM!
someone's poured gasoline over you,
thrown a match—
you're on fire!
and WHOOSH,
you're gone.

Maybe the fortune teller was right...
who knows?
But the next time your day feels
like empty space,
like you're not moving at all
and there's nothing in front of you...
don't blink.

LISTS

you made a list
and did the things on the list
and now the things on the list
are done

and tomorrow you will make another list
and you will do those things on the list
and then those things
will be done

while each day bleeds into the next

we were made for better than this—
we have these exquisite organs of
sense that can take us to the heights
of pleasure: color, sound, taste, smell,
touch, sex...

yet we move like slugs,
sliming our way through each day,
making lists...
lists!

how did we become
such horrible creatures?

we probably would inventory
the Garden of Eden

SEARCHING FOR ONESELF

So, according to the newspaper,
a busload of tourists in Iceland
stopped near a volcano crater,
and a women left the bus
to change her clothes and
freshen up,
and when she returned to the bus,
she was told that a woman was missing,
and she didn't recognize the description
of herself,
so she joined the search party.
Fifty people searched for hours,
a police helicopter was called in,
until somehow they finally figured out
that she was the missing person.

Isn't that life?
We're all in this huge search party
on the edge of the volcano
searching for ourselves
because we were told
we were lost.

RELATIONSHIPS

   I.
Ali was the toughest
criminal defense attorney I knew,
aggressive, sharp, hard.
Nothing could phase her.
All the judges were on their guard
when she was in court.
When the firm assigned
a new intern to her,
she was pissed.
"I don't have time for this," she said.
I was in her office the day
the new intern arrived.
She went out to the lobby
to get a look at him.
He was tall, blonde, blue-eyed, lean,
with a laid-back surfer smile.
She came back into her office
unable to breathe,
clutching her chest
looking at me wild-eyed,
"He's so handsome!" she gasped.

   II.
In Panamá there is a flower
called "Promise of a Man"
because its bloom
only lasts
for one day.

III.

Deborah was dating Rick while
she was married to Stephen.
After she divorced Stephen
she lived on his alimony and
continued to see Rick.
Rick had money but he was abusive.
She started dating Seth so she could
break up with Rick.
After she married Seth
she started dating Rick again.
She married Rick right after
she divorced Seth.
That was 3 years ago.
Now she emails Seth
about how abusive Rick is
and asks if Seth will
take her back.

IV.

Kristin was beautiful,
and knew it
(how could she not?)
Always dressed to kill,
flirted with every man she met.
the kind of woman who
would always check to see
if you were looking at her,

but always complaining
how she could never find
a decent boyfriend.

When I started dating her,
I found out why.

V.
Barry married Susan
because she got pregnant.
He swore he would divorce her
as soon as the daughter turned 18.

For the two years
after his daughter turned 16,
it was all he could talk about,
how he was going to
divorce Susan and be free.

That was about 15 years ago.
He's still married to Susan.

VI.
Carrie's husband was in Afghanistan
for two years.
She loved him so much.
She would come down to the bar
and play pool by herself every night,
and play their song on the jukebox
over and over.
She turned down every relationship,
but would sleep with someone
if it was totally no strings attached,
totally anonymous,
because in her mind
"that didn't count."
She and husband got divorced
about a month after he got back,
because she found out
he had cheated on her

VI.
Sheila texts me:
"I'm freaking out!
I wish you were here
so we could talk."

Although I was 3000 miles away,
I happened to be on my computer
and so I text back:
"What's wrong? Want to Skype?"

She texts back immediately,
"Yes, but I'm going to run first."

I respond, "Okay, text when you get back."

And she says, "Okay, but I'm taking
Grayson (her dog), so it'll be a while."

I respond, "Okay" but I didn't hear
back from her.

About 5 hours later I see that she
has posted several photos
of herself with her friends
on Facebook with the caption:
"Spending time with friends—
What a great day!"

VII.
The heart is a vessel that
is never filled.

The soul is a child that
is always lost.

The mind is a rumor
that is always wrong.

Relationships are masks.

THE HILLS GO BY LIKE YEARS

A woman sat next to me on the bus today.
That's how safe I now look!
She was a young woman,
and as she sat down she began to rummage
through her purse.
I knew what she was looking for, of course—
the ever present cell phone,
so she could listen to music
or scroll through Facebook
or text with friends she barely knows...
but as she was digging down in the purse,
her arm kept rubbing against mine.

She was an attractive girl—
I noticed her immediately
when she got on the bus,
and her arm was soft,
I could tell,
and it kept touching my arm
while she was so focused on finding
that damn phone.
I closed my eyes and let myself feel her touch.
I tried to take the feeling into my arm,
let it fill my body.
It relaxed me.
It was soft and warm and natural,
like dandelion seeds leaving the flower.

Finally she found her phone
and the touching stopped.
I stared out the window and
watched the hills go by like years.

I HOPE I MAKE IT

I hope I make it.
I hope I can pull this off,
make this work.
I hope it all comes together,
works out like I planned,
without fate, that evil twisted bitch,
sticking her hand into the future
and pulling the rug out
from under me.
And without death, that fucking heartless
bastard,
silently reaching in and
snipping the threads of life
by which we dangle so
precariously.

I hope I make it.
I've waited so long,
put up with so much,
just to get this far
and yet I'm still so far
so close and so far
from where I want to be.

All your meticulous plans
can go up in flames
with one match...
All the steps you took
can be washed away
by one unforeseen wave.

I don't deserve to make it.
I know that.
None of us do.
But I hope I make it,
and I hope you make it too.

PHALLUS IN WONDERLAND

It all seems to work so well
with no consequence to foretell,
when you're in that zone, or in that groove,
and your bodies seem to fit like glue.
That's how it is, that's how things stand
when you're cruising through Wonderland.

You meet a stranger in the park,
or in a bar, or in the dark,
or maybe it's just the girl next door
and you happen to knock upon her door,
but something magical and unplanned
always happens in Wonderland.

The air is hot or the air is cold,
and she slips off that bathroom robe
and lips and eyes and mouths collide
and suddenly he's inside.
And the sex is more than you both can stand;
that's how it is in Wonderland.

She's a beauty and he's well-hung,
or she's a virgin with a sapphic chum
or he's just young without a plan
when an older man lends a hand.
Gender's out and sex is in;
in Wonderland there is no sin.

But it never lasts more than a week,
maybe a month at its peak,
then comes pain, but no regret
'cause you go back every chance you get.
Love is good, but sex is grand;
that's how it is, in Wonderland.

WINTER FORECAST

Time falls like snow
and all history is slowly covered,
muffled,
and forgotten.
And the children of today look out
and see only the soft shape of hills,
not knowing the bodies that lie
beneath...
Erzurum,
Nanking,
Hankow,
Wormhoudt,
Malmedy,
Marzabotto,
Gardelegen,
Distorno,
Auschwitz,
Treblinka,
Simferopol,
Changjiao,
Odessa,
Bataan,
Rheinwiesenlager,
Hué,
Bengladesh,
Kenya,
Algeria,
My Lai,
Syria...

Time falls like snow, like a fine dust,
and all is obliterated, obscured,
forgotten, gone, never happened...

And the politicians can yap away
saying whatever they want
because no one remembers
all the corpses hanging from trees
or dumped into rivers
or tossed into the ovens
or bulldozed into ditches...
thousands and thousands
and millions and millions of
tortured, raped, mutilated,
murdered bodies...

Time falls like snow.
We can barely remember last year's
cell phone model...

The children sit on the floor
in one room playing Call of Duty
on the big computer screen,
while the adults sit in another room,
drinking,
and playing
Cards Against Humanity.

CRESTING THE HILL

The last time he saw her
she looked so sweet.
She said, "Don't worry Daddy"
as she kissed his cheek.
"I'm always careful, I'll be fine.
I'm meeting some friends
for a glass of wine."
She stepped out the door with a smile
and said, "I'll just be gone a little while."

The night was young with a hint of fall.
She met her friends at the nearby mall,
but their favorite club was a quarter-mile
so they walked along in single file.
They walked and talked as young girls will
as the drunken car crested the hill.

The impact hardly made a sound
as the drunken car left the ground
and went sailing up into the sky
and took her along for the ride,
and for a moment they hung in space,
two dancers caught in love's embrace.
That kind of love cannot be bound
but all the rest came back down.

When perfect storms seem to arise
survivors are left to agonize
if five minutes more or less
would have made all the difference
between two ships passing in the night
like distant dancing Christmas lights
or that dreadful knock upon the door
that alters everything forevermore.

NOBODY LIKES FISHBONES

Nobody likes fishbones in their oatmeal,
it's true.
Nobody likes fishbones in their oatmeal,
do you?

Everyone wants a wishbone in their life
Everyone wants a slave or a wife
Everyone wants someone with sex appeal
But nobody likes fishbones in their oatmeal.

I once had a girl who liked to play all night
I traded her for a twink whose ass was tight
It was never a case of preference
I just didn't see any difference.
Play all night or ass so tight
Everyone wants someone to feel
But nobody wants fishbones in their oatmeal.

We're all swimming in a sea of feel
Everything is sensual, nothing is real
And nothing really cures the blues
Like making love with someone new
A mound of flesh, a hank of hair
Someone to hold, someone to care
Someone to turn inside out
Someone to put inside your mouth.

For love is gentle when first it's new
But turns to bondage before it's through
So grab your straps while you're still young
And find some lass or a lad well hung
'cause when you're old and your head is gray
You'll find that no one wants to play.
And Life's buffet just has one meal:
Old fishbones in cold oatmeal.

MR. KURTZ, HE DEAD

If we could see how we end up,
we wouldn't even start...
That's why the gods invented time.
Time is Alzheimer's in reverse.
We simply have no recollection,
no clue, no memory, no idea
of the decrepit creatures we will become,
how we will live,
or how we will die.
But every day, a bit more of the memory
comes back to us,
and we get just a glimpse more
of what awaits us,
until finally
at the end,
we recall everything
in perfect
crystal clear
horror.

HEAVEN

Someone asked Jesus if
there was marriage in heaven,
and he said no,
that no, there was no marriage in heaven
but there was sex,
lots and lots of sex…
or maybe he said love,
that there was no marriage but
there was love,
but he meant sex,
lots and lots of sex…

I know this was what he meant
because it's the closest
I've ever gotten to heaven.

IN A RUT

There wasn't a time
when this particular future
didn't exist.

Remember playing alone on the hill,
under the tree,
watching the ants march through the grass,
then looking up to the blue sky
and wondering why you had no friends?

The ruts in the road
follow the wheels of the cart
and the cart follows the ox
and the ox follows the road.
You left home as a child
riding in the back of that cart,
and now you drive that cart
but the road is still the same
and you will ride in that cart
or drive that cart
in this life, and the next life,
and the life after that...

I wish I could tell you
that it was different.

I've tried all my life
to make it different
but I'm still on that same hill
watching
and
wondering.

SOUND CHECK

The kid who met me at the airport
was explaining what time the reading
would start and where it would be.
alder ash aspen birch buckeye
It was a small college in the Northeast
"I want to do a sound check
before the show," I told him.
buckthorn cedar chestnut cottonwood
"A what?" he asked.
"A sound check, you know, I want to check
the quality of the sound in the room."
cypress dogwood elderberry fir
"Well, there's just a microphone," he said,
"and a podium."
"I understand," I said, "but I want to do
a sound check. I brought a small in-line
modulator that I will hook to the microphone
and you can read a few lines and I will sit
out in the room and tell you how to set
the different levels."
elm fir hawthorn hazel hemlock
"It's just a regular microphone," the kid said,
"and they don't set it up until
right before the show."
"Well," I said, "they need to set it up early
so that I can do a sound check."
"Why?" he asked.
hickory honeylocus holly juniper
"Because," I explained, "in poetry,
sound is everything.
It's not the words
that have magic—
it's the sound of the words."
larch locust madrone maple

"I don't know if they can do that," he said,
"there's a rehearsal for Our Town
on that same stage right before your reading."
mahogany oak myrtle pine poplar
"Well," I said, "tell them to move the
motherfucking rehearsal!
I need the microphone set up
so I can do a sound check."
(I can be an asshole about these things.)
"Gee," he said, "I don't know."
redwood spruce sweetgum sycamore
"Look," I said, "if they give you any flack,
tell them to take a look
at the motherfucking contract.
No microphone check, no show, and they still
have to pay me. It's in my contract."
(I had learned to put that clause in there
several years ago.)

The kid dropped me off at my hotel and
ran off to find out about the sound check.
And while I was unpacking, I thought to myself,
"Nobody cares about precision anymore.
They just want get through the show so they
can write in their little alumni newsletter
that they had this person or that person
come to their little college so they can claim
what a big deal their little college is
so that they can ask for more money
from those same alumni.
But the thing is,
in poetry, sound is everything.
It's not the words that hold the magic;
it's the sound of the words."
tanoak walnut willow yew

TEACHING HORSES TO TALK

There once was a criminal
brought in chains before the king,
who sentenced him to death,
but the criminal said to the king,
"Sire, you have a horse,
and I could teach your horse to talk.
There is a stable at the jail.
Put the horse there
and let me work with horse for one year.
If I teach your horse to talk,
you set me free,
but at the end of a year
if your horse cannot talk,
you can execute me."
The king was intrigued, and agreed.
And every morning at the jail
the prisoner went to the stable
and talked at the horse all day.
After a few months, another prisoner
said to the man, "You are crazy.
You can't teach that horse to talk."
And the first prisoner said, "Maybe not,
but a year is a long time,
and many things can happen in a year:
I might die, or the king might die,
and you never know,
I might teach the horse to talk."

Thus I tell you: Persist in your folly,
be it music, art, writing, whatever,
because many things can happen in a lifetime:
you might die, or everyone else might die,
and you never know,

you might end up being a famous singer
or artist
or even a famous writer.

ASK SOMEONE WHO KNOWS

I don't understand how two people
can marry
and think that they will be happy
with only one other body to give them
each pleasure for the rest of their lives.
Anyone who's had a threesome
knows better.
Only one other body to kiss?
Only one other body to fuck?
Are you serious?
Anyone who's had a threesome
or a foursome
knows better.
You can take turns with multiple partners,
give yourself a rest,
watch and learn,
or do two-on-one, share the love
and the love making.
It takes all the pressure off you.
You don't believe me? Try it.
You'll never go back to monogamy.
I'm not trying to be blasphemous
or stir up trouble in happy marriages—
I'm just telling you how it is.
The night I watched her go down
and eat her girlfriend out, and then come up
and have both of them kiss me
before I went down on her too
stands as one of the best moments of my life.
It was that good.
It was better than Disneyland,
better than meeting the Dalai Lama,
better than winning a first class ticket
around the world.

Ask anyone who's had a threesome.
Male female female or
male female male or
male male male...
it doesn't matter... it really doesn't.
Any combination will work.
Isn't that odd?
Isn't it odd that gender stops
being an issue
when there's more than two of you?
You can't be homophobic when
there's a dick in your mouth,
and it's impossible to be anti-polyamorous
when you're watching two women
eat each other while you're kissing
breasts and feeling like you're the
luckiest man alive.

I know I know, you've all got stories,
stories of broken marriages,
stories of broken hearts,
and horrible jealousies.
Ok, I get that.
So don't do it.
I could be wrong.
After all, I'm no poster boy
for long-term relationships.
If you don't want to do it,
don't do it.

I'm just saying
I would do it again,
in a heartbeat,
and I only hope
I get that chance.

NAKED CITY

It's funny the sounds one hears at night.
No matter where one is in the world,
all night sounds are unanswered questions:
running feet down the street,
dogs howling in the distance,
car wheels going somewhere...
or nowhere,
or some crazed cranked-up meth head
walking down the street screaming
Fuck Fuck Fuck
at the top of his lungs...

It's like what the narrator said
at the beginning of that long ago
TV show:
"There's a million stories in the
Naked City... and this is one of them."
Except that the truth is,
there's a million stories in the
Naked City
and most of them are pretty pointless.

Still, I like the sounds one hears at night
I guess because I always like
unanswered questions.

It's the thing that keeps life interesting:
You never know how it's going to end,
because if you did,
you wouldn't bother with any of it.

Ah see? The dogs are howling again.
I wonder what they know.

ALL THERE IS

Martha was the kind of woman
who knew when to cut her losses.
We dated for a while,
and the sex was pretty good,
and I enjoyed her company,
but there was a certain
plateau quality to the relationship.
She was wanting a husband
and I wasn't so eager,
hence the plateau...
but the interesting thing was,
that when I told her
that I had met someone new,
bam! she was gone,
and I didn't hear a word from her
until about a year later when she
sent out wedding pictures
and was kind enough to include me
on the mailing list.

I always respect a woman who knows
when to cut her losses.
No point hanging around for love,
hoping things will work out.
Love is ruthless with us,
and we might as well be
ruthless with love.

THE AMERICAN HANDJOB

You know the handjob, the circle jerk,
the jack-off, the reach-around.
It's the sexual consolation prize.
It's what you get when the girl—or guy—
doesn't want to blow you.
It's the fourth place prize, the best effort ribbon,
The ho-hum, ok you can cum, throw away,
And it's a rip-off.
The hand jerk, the jerk-off, the pop-off,
the rub-out, the all-American handjob,
what the stripper gives you in the VIP room
for your $300,
or what the meth-masseuse gives you
for your $60
at the Happy Endings Massage joint.
It's the last sex you get from your girlfriend
before she breaks up with you,
or from the stranger at the bathhouse,
or from the old man in back of the porn store,
but it's better than being alone,
it's better than you doing it yourself
when you get home.
It's the all-American handjob con.
It's what you get when you turn on the TV.
It's what you get from the news.
It's what you get from the candidates.
It's what you get from your boss.
It's what you get from the real estate agent.
It's what you get from the lawyer.
It's what you get from the judge.
You're just one in a million, buddy.
Whip it out and stand in line.
Give them your money and be ready
with a Kleenex.
Here, let me wipe that cum off your pants.
Now, get outta here.

ME AND MARLON BRANDO

Me and Marlon Brando were having drinks last night...
of course, Marlon is dead, but nonetheless...
he was matching me drink for drink,
and the conversation turned to the topic of isolation
as it often does when I drink with Marlon,
and he was explaining how he got sick of Hollywood
and retreated to Tetiaroa
and I was sharing my similar retreats to places
somewhat less exotic,
and then he shared how terribly lonely it was
in paradise,
and I sympathized, because I understood.
He complained about the paparazzi.
Well, I couldn't match that, so I just nodded,
but then he complained about the lack of anyone
who understood him,
and I could certainly understand that,
and I shared how the cute lady at the dry cleaners
wouldn't even look at me,
but that didn't seem to match his stories about
Ava Gardner and Sophia Loren,
so I let him talk a bit more,
but the thing that really got me
was when he talked about killing himself
out there on his island off Tahiti.
He claimed he actually put the barrel of the gun
into his mouth, but didn't pull the trigger,
and he confided that the only reason he didn't
was because he couldn't stand to think
what the tabloids would say
about the rich Hollywood star
sitting on his own private island
off the coast of Tahiti who couldn't find happiness.
I topped off his whiskey and said I understood,
and that that was the exact same reason
that I couldn't pull the trigger either.

THE BLIND LOVING THE BLIND

I went down to the bathhouse today.
It took a 45 minute bus ride
plus a 15 minute walk
through crowded city streets
to arrive at a building with no sign
which is how bathhouses always are.
We outcasts find them on the web,
or by word of mouth,
and we enter silently
through the unmarked doors,
avoiding eye contact
while we wait in line to pay
the modest admission fee
and get our towels and locker key.
You can say what you want
about modern acceptance of gay culture,
but there's a reason why there's never
a sign on the bathhouse door.

I went down to the bathhouse today,
and the reason was simple: I was horny,
and by "horny" I mean "sexually lonely."
Many of the men who go to bathhouses
are married or otherwise encumbered,
but most of us are outcasts,
without partners,
alone in this world
with no one to hold them,
no one to touch them,
and by "them" I mean "me."
There've been brief affairs, here and there,
but it's been 3 years since a "relationship"
and that was with a married woman,
but I did love her, so it counts...

I went down to the bathhouse today.
I don't go every week, but certainly
every two weeks because
I love the steam in the dark room.
You can't stay in there too long
because it gets too hot,
and by "hot" I mean other men are
touching you
stroking you
and you are doing the same to them,
and it's completely dark
and you can't see any faces
or anything at all.
The blind loving the blind.
And after a while the heat gets to you
or the sex gets to you
and you have to step out
and jump into the swimming pool
with half a dozen other naked men
who are also cooling off
so they can go back into the dark,
the wonderfully dark,
the anonymously dark
steamy dark
steam room.
It's pitch black in there
and you are unencumbered
by anything that is "you" or
part of your life.
You are purely and totally anonymous.
You put one hand up to find the wall
as you slowly feel your way along,
and another hand up to find the wall
of flesh that is there in the dark,

and you encounter a bare chest
or shoulder, and you feel it gently,
and then you let your hand drop down
to find that cock,
be it hairy or shaved, large or small,
hanging or erect,
and sometimes it's already in
someone's mouth or in their hand
and if so, you reach further down
to feel the balls,
to give a helping hand, so to speak.
Sometimes it get so crowded in there
that you can't move, as hands grab
your cock, your butt, your asshole,
your nipples, all those hands,
passing you through the crowd
like an hors d'oeuvre tray that
everyone gets to sample, and
you are doing the same to everyone else.
Yes, the bathhouse is a marvelous place
for outcasts.
We can linger as long as we can stand it
although eventually all good things
must come to an end, or in this case,
end with a cum,
and finally someone strokes you over the edge,
or you do it to yourself while touching another,
and you cum,
and your cum falls to the steam room floor
along with all the other cum
of all the other outcasts,
a river of nepenthe
washed down the drain of absolution.
Outcasts come and go,
and after we cum, we go

out of the steam room doors to shower
and dress and return to a world that
doesn't really want us.

I went down to the bathhouse today,
took the 45 minute bus ride,
made the 15 minute walk,
paid my modest fee,
and went inside, stripped down,
showered in the wonderfully hot shower,
and went to the steam room,
but the steam room was closed for repairs,
which only left the swimming pool,
the hot tub, and a dry heat room,
none of which really work for outcasts
who need the anonymity of steam
and complete darkness,
and so, after walking around
for a dreary 10 minutes or so,
I went back to my locker,
put my clothes back on,
checked out, and returned to the streets
that really don't want me
and certainly don't need me,
and I made the 15 minute walk back
to the bus stop
to catch the bus home.

All of which goes to show
that even in paradise,
something is always fucked up,
even in an outcast's paradise.

HOME

"If I had the money," she says,
"I'd go back to California and try
and get my kids back."
I nod my head sympathetically,
and tell her I understand.
But I know there's no way.
She won't get the money,
and she won't make it back to California,
and even if somehow she did,
the state would never give those kids back to her,
kids who've grown up without her,
grown so much that they would be strangers now.
What do you say to someone
who thinks they've wandered
so far from home,
so far that all they can talk about
is trying to get back to a home
that never really existed,
or if it ever did exist
it's long since changed into something else.
What can you say except...
"I understand."

Because I do understand.
We've all wandered so far from our homes,
light years really,
and yet we still think we could go back
if only we had enough money
or time
or luck
or courage
but we don't have those things
and even if we did,

that home has long since changed into something else
and the people there would be strangers now.

No matter how much science fiction you read,
I'm here to tell you
that time only moves in one direction
and that direction
is away from home.

WHAT THE ANGEL TOLD THE LITTLE BOY

It's a very difficult thing
to occupy a human body.
We are not used to your form.
Our movements are gangly.
Coordinating two arms and two legs
is next to impossible for us.
Then we have to remember
all your routines:
when to wake up
when to pee
when to eat
how to say hello
when to say hello
when not to say hello.
But the worst part
is that we never feel
at home.
We always yearn to be
angels again,
to return to
formlessness
and lightness of being...
It's just so difficult to occupy a human body.

"Why do you do it then?"
the little boy asked.

The angel looked surprised.
"You keep asking us to."

JUST SITTING HERE THINKING

I was just sitting here thinking...
thinking about Jimmy Swaggart...
He was this famous southern preacher
(back when you were just a kid)
always preaching God's righteousness...
got caught with a prostitute
in a cheap New Orleans motel.
I think he paid her something like $15...
He got caught because another preacher—
whose name I forget—
was pissed that Jimmy had denounced him
for having affairs...
In other words, he had an ax to grind,
so the other preacher followed Jimmy
to the motel and took photos of him
meeting up with the hooker...
Anyway, the scandal went public
and Jimmy went on TV and cried,
and asked for forgiveness...
The hooker's name was Debra Murphree.
She got dragged into the spotlight,
was interviewed on TV talk shows,
and posed naked for Penthouse magazine
(that issue sold 4 million copies)...
Eventually Jimmy got his church back
but was caught with another prostitute
a few years later...
He's still preaching, of course,
although that won't last forever
(he's in his eighties now).
I don't know whatever became of Debra
but she will always be remembered
as the hooker who

brought down the preacher.
Anyway, I was just thinking about that.

And I was just thinking about
Monica Lewinsky...
She had a little fling with an important guy,
an important married political guy...
but Monica told the wrong people about it—
people who had an ax to grind,
and they exposed the little fling
for their own purposes,
and the newspapers had a field day
just like they did with Jimmy...
but the important man did his penance too,
and now he's back to preaching
although that won't last forever, either...
Monica had to capitalize on her
unwanted publicity too—
well, what else can you do?
If you're branded with a Scarlet A,
you might as well be brazen and
sell t-shirts with a big capital A on them.
She sold fashion items for a while,
and gave some good speeches
on the subject of shame.
I don't know how her life will turn out,
but she will always be remembered
as the intern who almost brought down
the President.
Anyway, I was just sitting here
thinking about that.

Sometimes one's choices are like tattoos.
It takes so little to be branded for life.
Fate simply extends an icy finger,

points at you and says "This one... let's make
an example of this one."
And the recipe for disaster is simple:
You just need a pound of weak flesh,
one ax to grind, one pinch of publicity...
Mix it up in a bored public fishbowl, and voila!
You're infamous for life.

And I was just sitting here thinking
about Amanda Knox.
She was just another American student
studying in Italy for the summer,
but the locals didn't like her antics,
partying in bars, and stealing local men...
(You can always pick out the Americans
in any foreign country—they're the loud ones,
the party animals, drinking or drugging,
having a good time, but always being
so blatant about it...)
so the locals had an ax to grind,
and the local prosecutor was ambitious,
and when Amanda's roommate
turned up dead, well... you know the story.
She did 4 years in an Italian prison
before the appeals court reversed her case
and set her free.
She returned to the US
and tried to live a quiet life,
but you know how it is,
so eventually she wrote a book
and made the talk show circuit.
A girl's gotta eat, you know.
She wasn't a murderer—she was just young
and got caught up in Fate's little recipe
of bad choices and unwanted notoriety.

I don't know how her life will turn out,
but she will always be remembered
as Foxy Knoxy.
Anyway, I was just sitting here,
just thinking about that.

One should try to learn from the mistakes
of others, but really, what can we learn?
The flesh wants flesh—you can't stop that—
and someone's always got an ax to grind—
there's no stopping that either.
So where's the learning?
Stay out of cheap motels?
Don't tell your secrets to your friends?
Don't party too loud?
Be discrete?
None of that will help you
if Fate decides that you're the one
it wants to have a little fun with
by nailing you to the cross
of public opinion.

So I don't have a moral here
or anything new to tell you,
I was just sitting here
thinking about these things.

DREAMING OF DINOSAURS

I have ice on my back, still stiff
from the drunken fall of two days ago.
Soon I will put on my coat,
lumber down the apartment stairs
to the dark rain-wet streets,
and walk downtown,
and select a bar to enter,
avoiding the ones too full or too empty,
and I will take my seat
and order a glass of wine,
vino tinto, as they say in my country,
red wine to carry me back
to memories of summers and women,
and the first sip will carry me there,
as it always does,
and at some point
(usually by the second glass)
I will wonder:
if someone were to scrape away
the dirt of who I am now,
could they,
by analyzing these scraps of paper,
these bleached word shards,
these fragmented thoughts,
could they reconstruct who I was,
and would they realize
that there was a time
when I was King?

ONE BECOMES ENCHANTED

One becomes enchanted by certain things...
It's an interesting word, "enchanted"...
meaning "delighted" or "charmed"
or more accurately,
"subject to magical influence."

One becomes enchanted by certain things...
a look, a smile, the touch of a hand,
the scent of perfume,
something that sweeps you away...
It's an interesting feeling,
to be enchanted by something,
or more accurately,
someone.

One becomes enchanted by certain things...
and you know it's illusional
and you know it's temporary,
and you just don't care
because you are transported
and transformed
and held aloft by the feeling
and you hope, against all hope,
that it's fate and that it will lead
to something wonderful.
It goes against all your experience
and all your logic
and all your justified cynicism
because you know how well-practiced
magicians can be in the art of
deception. Yet still...

One becomes enchanted by certain things...
like the way I was tonight
when you smiled at me.

ALICE'S RESTAURANT

Listening to Alice's Restaurant tonight,
recorded almost 50 years ago.
It's a fun, uplifting, song,
and I was remembering Woodstock
and Haight-Ashbury,
and I was thinking what a nicer time
it was back then,
but then I remembered
how many friends
I lost in the Vietnam War,
blown to bloody pieces by landmines,
or bullets, or shot down from the sky,
and the ones who came back
were maimed, amputated, crazed,
addicted, deformed, demented,
and how all of them simply disappeared
absorbed into history by PTSD,
ending up on street corners
holding cardboard signs,
or in hospitals (not VA hospitals
because the VA denied their claims),
or in jails,
or mostly dead, by drink or drug,
or by their own hand,
and it occurred to me
that nothing's changed.

Yes I was listening to Alice's Restaurant tonight
and I ended up feeling very sad,
and I thought about our current trough
of politicians, and I was reminded of
that last line in Easy Rider:
"We blew it."

Finally I put on Frank Sinatra
and poured a drink,
and then I felt better.

MY SECRET LIFE

Hanging on my wall
is a comic book cover
that I framed and put there.
The title "My Secret Life"
is written in huge letters across it,
and the picture, in bright primal colors,
shows a voluptuous blonde
on the witness stand
in a tight red dress
rising and pointing to the defendant
and saying something accusatory,
and the judge is pounding his gavel,
and the defense attorney has taken off
his glasses and is trying to stand up
to object to whatever the woman
is saying, but it's too late.

It's a great drawing, full of drama.

My secret life, however,
is much less dramatic.
Most people's secrets are that way:
less dramatic,
hardly worth noticing, really.
And yet, we keep our little secrets,
don't we?
We all have our Secret Lives,
and just like my framed picture,
they all bear the insignia of the
Comic Book Code of Approval.

PROGRESS

Another out-of-state developer came to town,
bought up this old historic building downtown,
kicked out the low-income tenants
who called it home,
and closed the bar on the first floor
that I called home,
and after some minor cosmetic touch-ups,
it'll reopen as subsidized senior housing,
and the developers will get lots of federal subsidies.
First they'll get a subsidy for preserving
an historical building, i.e., for not tearing it down,
and then they'll get another subsidy for converting it
to what they will call low-cost senior housing,
although it won't be that low-cost,
certainly not as low rent as it was for the 60
low-income folks who just got evicted,
and of course the developers will get some tax breaks
that they can use on their other investments,
and the management costs will be low because,
after all, seniors are easier to manage
than low-income folks,
and many of those evicted, because they're low-income,
are now homeless,
and the city will have to deal with them,
and my favorite bar
will reopen as a Thai restaurant or as an upscale
pizza brew-pub, and after a year, no one will remember
this dark gay bar that stood here for 42 years,
a place that so many of us called home.
The developers won't care, the investors won't care,
and the federal government won't even realize
that all their talk about preserving community is betrayed
by the very programs they fund.
That's "revitalization" of your downtown.
That's destruction of your community.
That's progress.

IT'S JUST SAD

That's how life is: just sad.
You get to a certain age
and it's just sad.
You go to some event
because some friends invited you
to go along,
and so you go along
and you have a glass of wine
or two.
It's okay wine, not great, but okay,
and there's some music playing,
it's kinda crappy but not too loud,
and you see some woman you know,
and so you go over to say hello
and you notice how much make-up
she has on
to cover up the years,
but you say hello
and you chat for a few minutes,
and you go back to your seat,
and have some more wine,
and you see some other woman
you think you know,
and you go over and say,
"Didn't you used to work at so-and-so?"
and she remembers you,
or claims she does, but nonetheless,
you are pleased she says that,
and you chat for a few minutes,
and then you go back to your seat,
and maybe have another glass of wine,
and the music gets loud,
too loud to talk,

and the younger people start dancing,
and you make your excuses to your friends
who invited you
and you walk home,
but it's still early,
and the woman with the too-much make-up
wonders "What's wrong with me?
Why didn't he ask for more?"
and the woman you used to know wonders
"What's wrong with me?
Why didn't he ask for more?"
And they both ask themselves,
if they've gotten too old,
but it's not them,
it's just you
and your sadness
walking home alone
to your apartment,
opening a nicer bottle of wine
and thinking how sad life is,
when you get to a certain age,
it's just sad.

BAMBI75

Bambi75 writes me and says she's waiting,
Kora25 says she's ready for a good time,
SuzySlut says she's hot and wet for me,
TamiMILF has enclosed pictures,
"Just click to open me,"
she writes in the subject line.

I'm sure the pictures are hot,
but I move TamiMILF into the spam folder
where she belongs
along with Bambi75, Kora25, SuzySlut,
and all the rest of today's offerings.
Manna from heaven I tell myself...
manna with barbed malware hooks
embedded deep within the folds of their
digital flesh.

But I think back to Ali...
She was also hot,
with concealed barbed hooks,
but at least her flesh was real,
and so we both clicked
on each other
for a while.

But a while was a while ago,
wasn't it?

Time is the spam folder of life.

GENTLY

Let me tell you how it is,
because no one else will:
We're all totally deluded.
Whatever you believe,
however you have constructed
your universe,
in whatever way you think
that you understand how things work...
you are wrong,
you are fucking wrong,
and the only thing that saves you,
is that everyone else is wrong too.
Whatever anyone tells you
about how things "really are"...
they are totally fucking wrong.
Just to be clear, let me repeat:
whomever you trust and rely on,
is fucked up...
the women you love,
the men you trust,
all fucking frauds, bless their hearts...
whatever you believe in,
especially if you believe it will save you,
is a totally fucking lie...
and whatever skill you have
in assessing the world
will not save you.
You have as much information
with which to make an informed decision
about the world as the ants crawling
down your wall,
which is to say,
zilch.

I'm just trying to break it to you
gently.

TAMMY

I was at this small wine bar Saturday night
when this man sitting next to me
started talking to me.
He was retired military, he told me,
and he looked it,
and he was there at the wine bar with his wife,
and sitting next to his wife was this woman
who was a friend of his wife.
The only reason I talked with this guy
was that the woman (the friend of his wife)
was kind of cute,
and without my asking,
he volunteered that her name was Tammy
and that she was not married.
Normally I don't like the name Tammy
but the month had been a bit lean,
and when I say the month, I mean the year,
and when I say lean, I mean bone dry,
so I chatted away with this guy
and stole glances at Tammy.
I would have guessed she was 48 or 50,
not by her face, which was wrinkle-free,
but by her neck and the skin that led
downward into her blouse,
so I deduced that she had had a facelift,
and in further chatting with this guy
I learned that Tammy had grown up in Altus,
halfway across the country,
and now worked at the nearby Army base
doing some kind of support thing for the troops.
The guy was a bit too friendly,
kept asking me questions about who I was,
what I did, etc., like he was vetting me,

like he was trying to hook me up with Tammy,
but I know where Altus is.
It's in Oklahoma, right next to the Air Force base,
and the only reason you grow up in Altus
is if your dad is in the military,
and now here she is, fifty years later,
working at a military base,
still trying to please her dad,
and the only reason you get a facelift
is to find a man,
and the only reason you go out with your
married friends to a wine bar on a Saturday night
is because you don't have a date
and your married friends take you out
to find you a date, and when I say date,
I mean husband.
So here I was being sized up
by this retired military guy,
and when I say guy, I mean pimp,
who was trying to pimp me out to Tammy,
so his wife would get off his back
about finding one of his friends
to take Tammy out,
because that's how married women are,
they want all their women friends to
get married too.

Now, I'm not unskilled at the art of conversation
so I chatted away with this guy,
acted all pro-military and all,
but I was losing interest fast,
and after the third drink, I made some excuse,
shook his hand, and said my goodbyes,
and he said how much he had enjoyed chatting
and I said that I came to this bar all the time,

and I was sure I'd see him again,
and as I walked out I made a mental note
never to come to this bar again.

He had no way of knowing, of course,
that the last thing I needed in my life
was Tammy
and certainly the last thing Tammy needed
was me.
I don't know why I've never liked the name Tammy
but I never have.
I suppose if she had been wearing a leather collar
and if the guy had told me she was a submissive
looking for a dominant,
or a dominant looking for a submissive
or a trans looking for some action,
maybe even a three-way with some DP,
I could have overlooked the name,
but I just have never liked the name Tammy.

METAPHOR METAMORPHOUS

I thought of a beautiful metaphor today
before my nap.
I was sitting at my desk
when it came to me.
It was this beautiful metaphor about
life and love and the futility of trying,
and I thought to myself,
"I should write this down"
but I wanted to play with it a bit more,
get it just right in my head.

It was the perfect metaphor for how
we always fuck things up,
how it's in our blood, under our skin,
like original sin…
we can't help but do wrong.
It's the knot we tie too tight,
the love we can't get right,
it's how we always aim for perfection
but like Icarus,
always in the wrong direction.
I should have written it down.
It was that good.
But I was tired and instead
decided to take a little nap,
and just like that,
my beautiful metaphor was gone.

Ain't that just like life,
to give you a beautiful metaphor
and then just snatch it away?

MINE FIELD

The barmaid was telling me about her third DUI
and how her probation officer didn't know
that she was a barmaid (which was forbidden),
and how her boyfriend was out of town
and she lived in a nearby apartment,
all mentioned, of course, in a casual way,
as she leaned over my table to refill my glass,
and then refilled hers, explaining that
she didn't have to pee in a cup for probation
until Monday, so she could drink tonight,
and then she told me about the two run-ins
with the cops she had recently,
and what assholes they were,
and how she told them off,
and then she adjusted her bra strap again
showing me more cleavage,
and said what a jerk her boyfriend was.
She was very entertaining,
in a fiery opinionated way,
using the word fuck often
as she ranted about various things.
She wasn't that young,
but she was still hot.

It was getting near closing time, and she gave me
a big hug (even though we had just met)
and I felt her warm body and I hugged her back,
and I considered
the following facts:
her ample breasts
her nearby apartment
her boyfriend out of town
her obvious flirting with me,

and compared them to the fact that she
was the kind of woman who liked to live
dangerously,
getting DUIs
lying to her probation officer
getting into arguments with the police,
and I considered that fiery temper of hers
and how everything that happened to her
was always someone else's fault.
I imagined her boyfriend showing up
just as I was spreading her legs
and her saying, "That bastard! He told me
he wasn't coming back until tomorrow!"
And I decided that it simply was just not
worth the risk
and I went home,
leaving her there to, no doubt,
blame me for failing to fuck her.

Some women are mine fields:
So hot in bed that they light a fuse
and just when you say "Be mine!"
they explode
and there you are—
riddled with shrapnel.

KILL FEE

A kill fee is what a publisher pays you
if they don't publish a story
that they asked you to write.
It's like a rejection letter with a check.
You invested all that time but they
just don't like the outcome,
so they give you a little something
for your time,
and then you simply go on to do
something else
with someone else.

My whole life is a series of kill fees.
It's what I got after my first divorce,
and after my second divorce,
and after this affair
or that affair,
or this job
or that job.
It's a little something for your time
so you can get on with life
and go do something else.

Time pays you a kill fee too,
after every year
you get a little something,
not much,
but a little something
for your effort,
so you can get on life
and go do something else
until you get the final
kill fee.

SOMEWHERE IMPORTANT

Darkness comes early this time of year
so it's especially important to get an early start
on this very important day,
but the highway is jammed already
because everyone else had the same idea,
so it's necessary to drive very boldly.
Luckily everyone else understands this as well
so the cops are letting everyone speed
because there are too many of us and
because they know that everyone has
somewhere important to get to
on this very important day.
But you need to make one stop at the liquor store
because you forgot to plan ahead,
and evidently so did a thousand other people,
because there are no parking spaces
so you park in the fire lane or the
the handicapped zone
like everyone else
and rush toward the store
past the ditched shopping carts
that litter the parking lot.
And inside the store it's worse.
Everyone's pissed off having to wait.
Can't they open up another check-out lane?
You curse yourself for volunteering to bring wine
to this important event,
and you curse yourself for not buying it sooner,
but finally you get your bottles and head out.
It's getting dark already
and you will need that drink tonight
when you make the first toast of the evening
wishing everyone a Merry Christmas.

ON WRITING POETRY

Most of the time you chase will-o'-the-wisps
reaching out for the right line
like a brass ring
that sings when it lands in your hand
and you try and write it down
before it slips away

but sometimes you catch one, like
"love is like giving a machine gun to a monkey"
and you sit there holding this thing
in your hand
just wondering
how the fuck you can work that into a poem
and you can't
so you discard it
and then later you think about it—
about how true it is:
Love *is* like giving a machine gun to a monkey...
but you still can't work that line
into a poem.

SEE YOU IN DREAMLAND

It's the world of dreams
that tells us what life means.
Do you think a split-open fig
could mean love or sex or temptation
without the meanings from the dreamland?
It's why thorazine makes patients
so flat, so one-dimensional,
so robotic, and so boring—
it's because the drug keeps them
from dreaming,
keeps them from filling their thoughts
with meaning, with hope, with love.
It makes them hollow, empty, dry vessels.

The dreamtime is where love comes from,
where water springs forth from rock,
where hope, fear, and flying all start,
where sex never ends,
and death never comes,
where animals talk, and spirits warn,
where nothing—and everything—is real.

When we arise in the dreamtime,
all the memories of our waking life fade,
evaporate into tatters and float away,
forgotten as a dream on opening day,
and the world before us is sequential,
consistent and totally logical,
as normal as apple pie,
until the alarm bell rings.

Each half of each day is spent in a world
where we are amnesic to the other half.
We are never truly awake,
never fully in touch.

CALLER ID

She called today.
I let the phone ring
and didn't pick up.

It's a mean thing to do
but I just couldn't bear having to
waste 30 minutes of my life
listening to her complain about hers.

She called today
and I thought about all the times
I needed her,
all the times I called her because
I was lonely or down or
horny or just needed to hear
a female voice.

I could have picked the phone up,
I should have picked the phone up,
because it really made no difference.

Either way
I felt crappy.

DIVERSIONS

Traveling is just a form of diversion.
Seen one castle? Seen them all.
Had one great meal? Had them all.
One more great wine? Why not?
But really, it's no different than the
fourteen year old kid with his face glued
to the iPhone iPad smartphone Xbox.
Something to keep us from experiencing
the present moment.
Ain't that the truth?
No one can stand being in the present moment,
doing absolutely nothing.

I'm no different.
My diversions might not be the same as yours,
but the goal is the same:
to fill up my senses as if I mattered.

We laugh at the video of the man
crossing the street, staring at his phone,
and getting hit by a bus,
but isn't that life?
We're all just crossing the street
completely distracting ourselves
while the bus turns the corner and
barrels down on us.

GALA

Adam and Eve took one tiny bite
of the knowledge of good and evil,
and the angels all freaked
and told God,
"Don't let them eat from
the tree of life,
or they will become like us."
So God kicked us out of Paradise.
(The angels have a strong union
and God didn't need any more problems.)

So all we know
is good and evil,
but that little bite of knowledge hasn't
done us much good,
has it?

We should have eaten
the whole apple.

OLD LOVE LETTERS

"How grateful I am for you in my life."

"You make me so happy and peaceful."

"My soul is full, full of love for you."

"Be patient with me, please."

There are several small boxes of these letters.
You read them and throw them away,
or rather, you start to throw them away
but decide to read a few,
but still you throw them away.

And you think:
one does not build a ship of death...
one empties out the ship of life,
box by box,
until the only thing left
is a thin hull.

R.I.P.

One less person I can write to.
I got the news Saturday.
We all did,
we, the still nameless invisible ones,
but he was one of us,
and for over 40 years a mentor to me
and an example to many
on how to gracefully live this life
which still has no name.
I know there are millions of us
but I only know a few,
only a handful
minus one now,
one less person I can write to,
one less person I can share the secrets
that those of us, whatever we call ourselves,
share with each other.

GHOST

All those who I've known
are dying now,
dropping like flies,
evaporating like disappearing ink,
leaving nothing behind.

It's a strange thing to live long
while everyone who gave your life
context
disappears.
Where, then, is the context?
If no one remembers that you won
the Pulitzer Prize,
the home run prize,
the hotdog eating prize,
then did you in fact ever win them?

You can't say to some young lady
over dinner,
"Did you know I won
the home run Pulitzer hotdog eating
contest in 1939?"
because, believe me, she doesn't care
and she doesn't even know
what they are.

Context is what gives our lives meaning.
Without it, we are ghosts.
Without someone to turn to and say
"Remember when we ate watermelon
by the river and Billy caught his hair on fire?"
it simply never happened.
Memories only exist when

the people you shared them with
exist.

I am a ghost now,
rattling these halls at midnight,
floating through these cities,
longing for a time when
someone remembered me.

SO MUCH FOR SINGULARITY

I'm a great believer in chaos,
not a fan, mind you, just a believer,
so all this talk about technology and
about how great the future
is going to be in twenty years...
well, I know we're just one nuclear attack
or one massive organized computer hack
away from the stone age...
I mean, you can run all the numbers you want,
do all the math and all the data extrapolation,
and a roomful of quants can prognosticate
the future growth of the exponential
technology explosion,
but I've spent too many years playing craps,
so I know how math really works.
Just when you think you can't possibly
roll a 2, 3, or 12
thirty times in a row...
you will...
and your bankroll is completely wiped out.

It's no different than the quants who programmed
the giant Wall Street computers to trade
a million synthetic derivatives in microseconds
based on certain market assumptions they made,
and when those assumptions turned out to be
wrong,
the bankrolls of a million pensions were wiped out
in one day.
Who could have foreseen that so many
credit default swaps would come due at once?
The same people who didn't foresee thirty rolls
of 2, 3, and 12.

"The future looks brilliant" is what
Thomas LaMont, the head of J.P. Morgan,
told Herbert Hoover five days before the 1929
market crash.

Programs fail, computers fail, companies fail,
and technologies fail for the same reason
that humans fail: hubris.

I've got nothing against computer technology.
I use it all the time,
and I'm sure it will continue to grow exponentially,
with or without us,
and do great things,
with or without us.
I'm just saying that there are other technologies
that are growing just as fast,
such as the randomness of Shiva,
the chaos of Maha Kali,
and of course, the best one of all:
Thanatos,
man's ability to fuck everything thing up.

And if not economic or technological collapse,
then certainly we're all just
one heart attack away from nothingness,
and that's the only singularity
you can count on.

GENESIS

It was a dusty day in the universal void
and God sneezed
and thousands of God's tiny water droplets flew
out into space
and got covered with dust
and became planets.

All this cosmic spinning around
and personal angst about
the meaning of life
simply because God forgot
to cover his mouth.

THE HARDEST PART

The hardest part is the beginning.
You don't know where to go,
but you just have to start somewhere,
and once you start, well then, at least
you're on a journey going somewhere.
Most people fail because they never start.
They're afraid of making a mistake.

The hardest part is the middle,
because you will have to change course.
I guarantee it.
Something will happen and you will realize
that you're going the wrong way,
and you must change course.
Most people fail because they refuse
to change direction.
They're afraid others will judge them.

The hardest part is the end
because no matter where you end up
it's never quite how you thought
it would be, and you will need to
accept that, and enjoy what is there,
because there isn't any more time.
Most people fail at the end because
they become bitter, and they are bitter
because all along they thought they
were entitled to great rewards.
There are no great rewards.

But life is not failure.
Not starting is failure;
Not changing is failure;
Not loving what you end up with
is failure,
but life is not failure.

FROM WHOSE BOURN

There is this island, you see...
or rather, that I see...
off there in the distance
under low clouds,
further away than it looks
but closer than you think.

It's strange to think of one's own death.
No matter how you try,
you can't get your head around it
and finally you are left with only one hope—
that you don't die stupidly...
trying to get the toast out of the toaster
with a knife,
or crossing the street without looking...
You just don't want your last thought to be
"Fuck! That was stupid!"
or
"What a waste!"
even though
ultimately
we all end up thinking
one or the other.

GOD'S PLAN

Two nice young men
came to my door the other day,
and told me that God had a plan for me,
and I said, "Yes, I know,"
and then they said that they
wanted to be a part of God's plan for me,
so I asked them if they liked
having sex with men,
and they both looked shocked and said "No."
So I said "Well, then I guess you can't be
a part of God's plan for me,"
and I closed the door.

The next day, one of the nice young men
came back to my door,
and told me he had changed his mind
and wanted to be part of God's plan for me,
so I let him inside.

God moves in mysterious ways, you know.

LIFE BREAKS EVERYONE

Life breaks everyone.
That's what Ernest Hemingway said,
and I have found it to be true.
When you're young you don't believe it
but when you're older... you do.
Life breaks everyone.
Hemingway claimed that some people
were stronger at the broken places,
but I have not found that to be true.
It certainly wasn't true for him.
Is it true for you?
Life breaks everyone
either dragging you slowly over the years
wearing you down with sandpaper blues
or snapping you suddenly
with horrible news.
Life breaks everyone.
It's been true for me.
Has it been true for you?

STREET LEGAL

Love is a two-way street, they say.
What they don't tell you
is that everyone is going ninety mph,
and all the signal lights are out,
and no one obeys them anyway
because no one has any brakes.

It takes two to tango, they say.
But no one tells you it takes three to foxtrot
and four to really fuck things up.

I never promised you a rose garden, they say.
But you didn't expect all thorns, did you?
You thought there might be a hint of rose,
a few soft petals.

You can't fight city hall, they say.
But no one told you that city hall would
shoot you for trying.

It's a jungle out there, they say.
Well... they were right about that one.

Love is a two-way street, they say.
But you are just a pedestrian
and as you get older you find
there are no more sidewalks,
not even a shoulder.

Love is a two-way street,
littered with total wrecks,
broken axles, broken glass, broken hearts,
and not everyone walks away.

SHRUNKEN HEADS

I keep a gaggle of shrunken heads
tied to my belt
the way other people keep appointments.
It's my abacus of time.
I rotate them from belt loop to belt loop
like planets circling the sun
to mark the passage of the years.
There used to be lovers' heads hanging there
tied together by long hair,
but now it's just doctors, specialists,
accountants and lawyers
attached by dollar bills and fear.
I preferred the shrunken heads
of lovers—even with their eyes sewn shut,
they would still try to kiss my thigh
below where they were tied,
but the banker heads have tiny teeth
and they just try to bite
and the accountants never shut up
and the lawyers, well, they just lie.
It's a crappy way to mark the passage of time
using shrunken heads as a type of sundial.
After a while the heat gets to them,
and they all begin to stink.

GHOSTS FROM THE FUTURE

I told her I was a ghost
from the future
come back to warn her.
She didn't believe me, of course,
and went on with her life
repeating the same patterns
over and over,
the way we all do.
Of course, I'm not a ghost
(at least, not yet)
but you don't need to be a ghost
to foretell someone's future—
you only need to listen to their story
and extrapolate out about twenty years—
everyone tells you their future
because no one ever changes.
Life is just rolling the same hoop
down the street over and over.

Anyway, I had only known her
about six months
when I gave her that line
about being a ghost,
and then I vanished from her life.
That was ten years ago
and she had just turned thirty.
I haven't seen her since.

She was the kind of woman
who packed three suitcases for a weekend visit
because she had to have enough outfits
to always look stunning.
And she did always look stunning.

She had hundreds of clothes
and two closets full of shoes.
She was obsessed with looking beautiful.
I tried to tell her that beauty and style
weren't everything,
but at thirty she only laughed at me
and said I was a strange fellow
and was just being negative.

As I say, it's been ten years
since I've seen her
but last month, I got an email from her.
She has turned forty,
and she wrote me to say
that she is aging and hates it,
that she exercises furiously every day
to keep her figure,
and that she dates furiously too
but just can't seem to find the right man.

I remember how, ten years ago,
all the men pursued her.
Every man in town was in love with her.
I know, because I was too.
She drove around town
in that cute little sports car
waving and laughing as she sped by.
She dated furiously back then too
but could never seem to find
the right man.

You see how the hoops repeat themselves?

And as for me, well... I've rolled my hoop
a little further down the road too.

I live in another country now.
I am an *extranjero* here,
a foreigner, a stranger,
wandering through these Latino streets,
but I was an extranjero ten years ago too
when I wandered into her life
the way that ghosts do.

I told her I was a ghost
come back from the future,
but now, I think of her as a ghost.
Isn't that how we always think
of the people we've loved
and of the people who've loved us?
They're all ghosts now.
All we have are a few images in our minds
or the occasional strange apparition
in dreams.

In her email, she said
she wanted to see me again,
that she really missed me,
and when I read that
I toyed with the idea
of actually going to visit her,
but I dismissed it,
because to see her again,
to see what she's done
with the past ten years,
how well, or poorly, she's aged,
how much, or little, she's learned
means I would have to examine
my own past,
and none of us want to do that,
do we?

None of us want to have
that little chat with ourselves.

We pass through each other's lives
like ghosts, don't we?
Or maybe it's our own lives
that we pass through.
Maybe we're all ghosts from our own future.
We've come back to warn ourselves,
but we never listen,
do we?

THE PRICE OF PARADISE

Paradise is not for everyone.
Remember, even Adam and Eve bolted
from the Garden after two weeks.
No, paradise has its drawbacks...
For one thing, it's just paradise,
so it's perfect, which sounds nice,
but that means there's no variation.
It's like finding the perfect soul-mate...
Go ahead, get married,
stay married for twenty years,
listen to the same old stories
the snoring
the occasional vanilla sex...
and eventually you'll be checking the ads
for a divorce lawyer, or an affair,
or both...
Yes, variety may cause most problems
but it's also the spice of life.
If you're on the perfect beach
with nothing to do all day long
and the bar serves the perfect piña colada,
but only serves piña coladas
and nothing else,
well, after a while, you get sick of sugar
and sick of perfect sunsets...
And this is true not only of places
but of life itself.
Isn't being alive the ultimate paradise?
Feeling, seeing, tasting, kissing, eating,
moving around in time and space
with different things happening every day...
Isn't that paradise?
And yet, we grow tired of that too,

and do our best to find the exit,
just like Adam and Eve did
so many centuries ago.

I LEFT THE BAR

I left the bar because it was empty.
I can be alone at home,
and the wine is cheaper,
and the conversation more intelligent.

I left the bar because it was empty,
except for one guy down at the end
who kept trying to chat up the waitress.

I left the bar because it was empty,
except for that couple who were obviously
in love with other, or soon would be.
If there's anything worse than people in love,
it's people who are about to fall in love.

I left the bar because it was empty.
The band was just setting up and wouldn't start
for another hour,
and I could tell they were going to be loud,
and if there's anything worse than loud,
then it's a crowd.
And if there's anything worse than a loud crowd,
it's a loud crowd of people in love
or about to fall in love.

I left the bar because it was empty.
I've been in this town for two months
and I haven't met anyone yet.
What's wrong with people?

GEOLOGY 101

People are like geological layers:
The first thing you see is appearance,
maybe green grass,
a well-manicured lawn
or wild amber waves of grain
or an overgrown thicket of sharp thorns
or a vast and vacant desert,
but it's always interesting...
first appearances are always interesting.
But peel back that thin layer of appearance
and you find the crust of people,
the hard dull heavy thick personalities
fractured by internal pressures
created eons ago deep inside them.
The crust wraps around us
Like a perpetual nail gun
and ultimately, it's boring.
You start to get to know someone,
realize they're just crusty,
and you stop wanting to know them.
Crusty people are boring.
But, peel back that crust, and reach down
and you come to the mantle, way down,
way way down inside, under all that crust,
is the mantle, hard as diamonds, full of iron.
That's where people get their strength.
That's what holds up the crust,
keeps the earth from exploding
from all the internal pressure.
Crusty people are only thirty miles thick,
paper thin really,
but the mantle is eighteen hundred miles thicker.
It's our backbone, our skeleton,

our hardheadedness that makes us keep going
when it's all so pointless...
And if you are ever so lucky as to peel back
someone's mantle,
then you find their core,
that white hot plasma of pure energy
pulsating, bubbling, burning—
pure fucking energy!
Everything that makes being alive
so real, so important, so precious
is because of our core.

But wait, there's more!
If you could get through someone's core...
which you can't...
but if you could get to the very center
of someone's core,
you'd find their inner core,
something so rare
that no one knows
what it is.

So the next time you see some
well-manicured lawn walking around
or some crusty old geezer sitting on a bench,
just remember:
somewhere under that thick mantle
is a burning hot soul
just wanting to explode.

THINK ABOUT IT

Did you ever notice
how no one ever wants to exchange
their life for someone else's?
People love to complain, but when you ask
"Who would you rather be?"
they can't name anyone.
I mean, think about it.
Is there anyone else you would rather be
than yourself?
If Jesus came back to earth,
or some fantastic space creature from
another planet,
or a genie from a magic lamp appeared
and said, "You could be anyone else,
anyone else that you want right now,
I will make you that person right now,
but you have to stay that person"—
How many of you would do it?
Who among you would do it?
I wouldn't.
There's no one I'd rather be in this world
than me.
I mean, THINK about that.
What does that mean?
I mean, I know life sucks—
my life sucks—
but how bad can it be
if I won't change places with ANYONE
on this earth.
Think about that.
Ain't that weird?

WHISPERS

Do you know why God only speaks
to us in whispers?
It's because his voice is shot
from centuries of shouting,
so all he can manage now
is the barest of whispers.
In another thousand years,
his voice will be completely gone
and there will only be silence
and the people
—if there are any people left—
will think that God has abandoned them.
But God has never abandoned us...
You just have to listen
very
very
carefully
to hear him now.

ANOTHER DAMN POEM ABOUT LOVE

Love is a lottery ticket.
What are the odds?
But you play anyway.
Life is a drawer
full of old lottery tickets
that didn't pan out,
each one a springtime of hope
in its day.
And there's nothing like hope, is there?
Besides, it's only a dollar... or two
and what's a dollar for a springtime of hope?
So you go down to the corner store every day,
or the corner bar every night,
still betting those same old numbers.
It's only a dollar.
Think of the memories you're buying.
But every night around 8 o'clock
the numbers are drawn
and someone else gets lucky,
so now you've got a drawer full of memories.
That's all life is, you know...
a drawer full of memories.
Sometimes you pull one out and look at it
and try and remember
that particular combination.
It was a warm sunny day, remember?
And you were feeling particularly lucky,
remember?
When you threw down your dollar
and said to the man behind the counter,
"I'll take a quick pick."
Remember?
Love is a lottery ticket.
Somebody's got to win,
and you can't win if you don't play.

WHAT MARK RUDD DREAMS

If you think that right is on your side,
you're probably wrong.
If you think that God is on your side,
you're definitely wrong...
It's only when people think
they're on the moral high ground
that they do terrible things.
Let me tell you about me...
I came of age during the Vietnam War
and the Vietnam War made us all crazy
because everyone was being drafted
to fight in a war that made no sense.
58,000 Americans died in Vietnam,
and the ones who didn't die came back
as junkies or crazy or both.
We all thought the world was insane.
There were protests in the streets
every single day,
but they made no difference
because the American government thought
it was on the moral high ground.
So the protesters turned violent
and buildings were bombed
because the protesters thought they
were on the moral high ground.
Remember the Weathermen?
They bombed the U.S. Capitol in 1971;
They bombed the Pentagon in 1972;
They bombed the U.S. State Department in 1975;
And in 1981, they robbed an armored truck
and stole $1.6 million and killed two police officers
and a Brinks guard.
It's only when people think

they're on the moral high ground,
that they do terrible things.

Oh wait...
You don't remember the Vietnam War?
Or the Weathermen?
Well, okay, what about Timothy McVeigh?
He thought he was justified blowing up
a federal building in Oklahoma in 1995,
killing 168 people.
He felt he was on the moral high ground
because he was protesting what the FBI did
when they blew up a building
held by the Branch Davidians
in Waco, Texas, killing seventy-eight people.
The FBI felt they were justified
because the Branch Davidians refused to
obey a search warrant.
And of course, the Branch Davidians felt
they were justified because they were just
practicing their religion
and didn't need to obey the government.
It's only when people think
they're on the moral high ground,
that they do terrible things.

Oh... you don't remember Waco
or Timothy McVeigh?
Oh... okay... well, as I said,
I came of age during the Vietnam War
and the Vietnam War made us all crazy
and I was getting
conscientious objector status counseling
at my church
because, you see, you had to document

that you had received years of church counseling
to qualify for a conscientious objector deferment
to the draft.
It was a religious deferment, you see,
and I was fourteen years old,
and I was going to a church I didn't believe in
to get counseling for something
that should have been obvious
because I needed that documentation to apply
for a conscientious objector deferment
four years later when I turned eighteen
and had to register for the draft,
because I didn't want to kill anybody,
and at fourteen I couldn't tell my parents
because they worked for the same government
that was promoting the war
that I wasn't going to fight in.

So I went to church
and buildings were bombed
and protesters were murdered
and police were murdered,
and the war went right on.

Jeffery Miller, Sandra Scheuer,
and William Shroeder were three students
murdered by the National Guard at Kent State
during a protest of the U.S. invasion of Cambodia;
Peter Page, Edward O'Grady, and Waverly Brown
were three police officers murdered
by the Weathermen in New York.

It's hard to tease out what was right from
what was wrong about the Vietnam protests.
The war ended over forty years ago,

and Vietnam is a big tourist attraction now,
and the only thing I've learned in those forty years
is that the moral high ground
is as slippery as wet ice
and everyone who climbs up there
pays a terrible price.

So I wonder what Mark Rudd dreams about,
and what Bernardine Dohrn dreams about,
and what Linda Sue Evans dreams about...
Do you remember them?
They were part of that Weathermen group
that did terrible things
because they believed
those things would help stop a terrible war.
It's okay that you don't remember them.
It was forty years ago.
They're all out of jail now,
leading normal lives,
and they probably don't think much of us either.

But I wonder what they dream about,
and I wonder at what point is it okay
to do terrible things to protest
the terrible things that other people do.

I still don't know.

So now, forty years later,
the only truth I have found
is that terrible things
always come
from the moral high ground.

LONG (STARRY STARRY) NIGHT

This is going to be a long night.
I can tell.
I only have one box of wine,
and it's a small one-liter box
which is both a good and a bad thing.
Good, because I won't be that hungover
tomorrow.
Bad, because I won't be that drunk tonight.
But I might as well get started,
so here's my first glass.
Mmmm, not bad for a box wine.
I'd better write a note to myself
to buy another one tomorrow,
maybe two,
because they're small.
That's one thing about being older—
you write yourself a lot of notes.
The wind is blowing hard tonight.
There are no clouds in the sky,
and I can see stars.
I think of Van Gogh
who sacrificed so much for his art.
He was a better man than me,
but then, many men are better than me.
I do what I can.
Van Gogh painted almost nine hundred paintings.
Nine hundred!
He only sold one in his lifetime.
I've written a dozen books or so,
and I've sold a few, one or two,
but then again, mine are priced at two dollars each.
Quite a bargain.
I wonder what Van Gogh sold his painting for?

Whoever bought it got quite a bargain too.
It's going to be a long night...
It was a long day.
I spent the day writing, or rather, proofreading.
I proofread sixty-eight pages of this novel I'm working on.
I wrote two new pages.
Now I have seventy pages.
It's a slow process.
Van Gogh was prolific.
He often painted two pictures a day.
I wrote two pages today.
I'm not prolific.
For me, writing is a slow process.
I write more when I'm drinking.
That's my motto, you know:
Write drunk; edit sober.
That's one thing I think I have
that Van Gogh didn't have—
a sense of humor.
I don't think Van Gogh ever said to Gauguin
"Friends, Romans, countrymen,
lend me your ear."
But then, Van Gogh didn't have the internet
where he could peruse millions of jokes.
When I was in Amsterdam,
I went to the Van Gogh Museum.
It took my breath away.
And I went to the Anne Frank House.
It took my heart away.
We simply don't know what suffering is anymore.
We've been immunized, inured, buffered,
swaddled, fattened-up, and dumbed-down...
We have no idea what suffering is.
There's no more working class,
no more citizen class,

just consumers.
I read somewhere that Van Gogh drank Absinthe.
I don't know if that's true.
I drink boxed red wine.
Here's my second glass.
I usually get about three glasses from a liter box,
three big glasses.
It's going to be a long night.
My friend Marco just texted me.
I think he's been drinking too.
He's a bit younger than me
and cute,
actually quite a bit younger than me
and very cute.
Evidently this is very good red wine
because I've texted him back and offered
to take him to a hotel this Friday.
Such is life.
Van Gogh was straight, I believe,
so his options were limited.
Such is life.
I'm bi, so my options are wider, but
I'm also older which limits them.
Such is life.
Hmmm Marco has written back
and accepted my offer.
I'd better write myself a note
so that tomorrow I will remember that
tonight I committed to book a hotel room
for young Marco this Friday.
Oh my
bump
       bump
              bump
down the funny stairs.

What a strange life this is.
I just don't understand life.
One moment you're lonely and alone
thinking that the sadness will never end
and the next moment you're making a date
to fuck the cutest boy you've ever met.
It just makes no sense.
The history books say that Van Gogh
used to frequent the hookers.
Maybe he felt the same longings I do.
Maybe he made dates to do things
the same way I do,
feeling the same anticipation.
Sex is the color of life, is it not?
The starry of the starry starry night?
Well, I don't know.
I've poured my final (big) glass of wine
and tossed the empty cardboard box
into the trash.
I'm actually quite fond of Marco.
I've taken him to hotels before.
He's a good lover.
This is a good wine.
I really have no idea what suffering is.
I mean, I do what I can with words.
I crank out the pages every day,
and I won't cut my ear off for any hooker,
well... not anymore anyway...
but I have no idea what suffering really is.
I have no idea if my art
is really art
or just my ejaculating all over the page.
It's going to be a long night,
but fortunately
the edges are starting to numb.

METAPHYSICS

If you look at something long enough, you become that thing. This is a concept that is very hard to grasp, because it seems so improbable. You say, "If I stare at a door for a long time, I do not become the door." But in fact, you do. If you stare at a door long enough, you become a doorway. You start thinking about opening and closing, coming and going, locked doors and open doors, opportunity knocking at the door... You start thinking about opening that door that has so long seemed closed, maybe even stepping through that doorway and stepping down a different path in life.

If you stare at a rock long enough, you become solid, hard, compact, heavy, powerful, immovable. You start thinking about taking a stand against the soft earth, against the multitude of soft opinions, against the noise. You become silent, implacable, merciless, unyielding. You start thinking of outlasting all your enemies simply by doing nothing but enduring. You start thinking about the art of doing nothing.

If you stare at the sky long enough, you become light as air. You float like the breeze, like clouds. You fall like rain. You rise like mist. You shapeshift to fit any obstacle, any opponent. You conquer by drifting.

If you look at something long enough, you become that thing.

DIVORCE

I loved her.
I suppose, on some level, I still do,
or at least, I understand her.
I married her.
We divorced eight years later.
We still keep in touch
although it's been ten years
since the divorce.
Our emails tend to dwell on
the little bit of common ground
that still remains:
updates on people we knew,
how the farm is doing,
her current husband's health,
her health...

Here's a sad fact about divorced couples:
One of them will die before the other,
and the one that remains will always wonder
what it would have been like if they had
stayed together.

Here's another sad fact about divorced couples:
Most of them needed to divorce.
It's hard to be a couple.
People wear out.
People wear each other out,
and time wears everyone out.
Time, external circumstances, and of course,
hardness of heart.

They say that divorce
is the worst experience in the world,

more stressful than when your parents die—
and that certainly was my experience.
The pain lasted a long time,
and sometimes, even after ten years,
if I think about it too much,
it still hurts.
But I got on with my life,
and she got on with hers.
That's what divorced couples do.
You get on with your life,
because you have to.

You get on with life
and never talk to your ex again
or you stay in touch
and send little emails now and then
because maybe
despite time
and external circumstances,
your heart isn't completely hardened.

Here's another fact about divorced people.
Most of them marry again.
She did.
I didn't.
No particular reason—I just didn't.
Maybe the gods were tired
of fucking with me,
or maybe I was just lucky,
or just unlucky.
I can't decide.

Some people just aren't cut out
to be married,
and I didn't know that about me

until I got married.
So now... I'm divorced.

I'm not expecting love to find me again.
I'm old and cranky and set in my ways,
but if it did,
I hope I would try to be a kinder person.

THE FUTURE

Listening to the old men at the bar
talking about the future.
One says, "They're gonna cut Social Security
twenty-five percent in ten years."
The other answers, "In ten years I'll be eighty-two or
in the ground. Either way, I won't care."
The third one says, "Eighty-two? I didn't think
you were that young."
The first ones says, "Ten years...
just think about it..."
"Yeah," the second one says,
"Nothing to look forward to except pussy."

LAW OF THE JUNGLE

Do you blame the cat
for catching the mouse?
Do you criticize the lioness
for eating the antelope?
Or the termites
for eating the wood?
No.
You say it's in their nature,
Survival of the fittest,
Natural selection,
Law of the jungle...

Well, isn't the same true for tapeworms?
Do you blame them
for looking for a host?
Laying their eggs in some fish
that ends up on your sushi
and then in your gut.
Attaching the tiniest teeth
to your intestines
hoping for a little manna
from the heavenly host,
a little of your excess blood
that you'll never miss.

If you don't blame the mouse-catcher,
then you can't blame the tapeworm.
It's in his nature to feed off you,
to corrupt your internal workings.
And if you can't blame the tapeworm,
then you can't blame the politician.
It's in his nature to feed off you.
He has no choice.
He too was born with
tiny teeth
with sharp points.

BEFORE MATH

Catalina is so upbeat. When I say I'm down,
she suggests I just go to a bar and meet people.
She doesn't see the math.
She's thirty.
When she goes to a bar, she meets people.
Everyone looks when she walks in.
Everyone wants to talk with her.
But me?
I'm staring down the seven-aught barrel of time.
When I go to a bar, no one looks up.
No one wants to talk to me.
I'm just the old man at the end of the bar.

But that's why I enjoy talking to Catalina.
She reminds me of how sweet life used to be,
before math...
how eyes used to look at me,
acknowledge me,
when I walked into a bar
or just walked down the street.

I don't have the heart to tell her about math,
about the arc of youth, the parabola of time,
the calculus of diminishing returns,
and the spiritual meaning of zero.

So I keep my mouth shut about math.
I don't want to be too negative, you know.
If there's anything worse than an old man,
it's a negative old man.
And if there's anything worse
than a negative old man,
it's a negative old mathematician.

HISTORY LESSONS

Remember history class in school?
I hated history class,
memorizing all these dates
about things I didn't care about.
1215 the Magna Carta
1455 the War of the Roses
1815 the Battle of Waterloo
Who cares? I didn't.

But now I read history and I'm amazed.
It's like looking into a crystal ball
and seeing the future,
except the future is just the past
repeating itself over and over.

You look at today's situation and you think that
this is the first time someone got to be a leader
simply by the force of their personality?
Shit, dude.
Here's a quote. See if you can guess who said it:
"What this country needs is a man ruthless and
energetic enough to make a clean sweep."
Give up? It's our old friend Benito...
Benito Mussolini.

So sit back and relax
while all hell breaks loose
and a police state is imposed
and the constitution is shredded.
We can rewrite it when we emerge
from the ashes of the next holocaust.
Humanity's been through this before.

Do you know why Jesus said

the meek will inherit the earth?
Because the meek don't win elections.

Here's the history that should be
taught in school:
37 Caligula
81 Domitian
198 Caracalla
235 Maximinus Thrax
284 Diocletian
434 Attila
690 Wu Zetian
1099 Godfrey of Bouillon
1206 Genghis Khan
1370 Timur
1509 Henry VIII
1533 Ivan IV
1644 Chang Hsien-Chung
1793 Robespierre
1865 Leopold II
1917 Lenin
1922 Stalin
1922 Mussolini
1933 Hitler
1939 Franco
1949 Mao Tse-tung
1971 Idi Amin
1973 Pinochet
1975 Pol Pot
1979 Saddam Hussein
1980 Robert Mugabe
1992 Radovan Karadzic
1994 Kim Jong-il
2000 Bashar al-Assad
2011 Kim Jong-un
2016 Trump

THE THINGS ONE LEARNS

"The things one learns," he said,
"are learned too late to be useful."
We were sitting on a park bench
waiting for the sun to get past the trees
so its rays would warm us.
I had brought him a cup of coffee
which he held in torn-glove hands.
"I could have married Mildred," he said.
"I should have married Mildred,
but I went to San Diego for a job.
I thought it would make me rich...
They sent me to New York,
and then to Chicago.
Then they went bankrupt,
and left me stranded in Chicago.
By the time I got back to Montana,
she was gone..."
"How long ago was that?" I asked.
He looked away and thought.
"About 50 years ago," he finally said.
"Did you ever get rich?" I asked.
"Just once," he said,
"but I spent it all... It all seems
so stupid to me now,
but there was a time when I thought
that a good job and money
was more important than love."
"The things one learns," he repeated,
"are learned too late to be useful."
The sun made it over the trees
and the warm rays felt good.
"Where are you sleeping?" I asked.

"At St. John's," he said, "on a cot
in their basement with twenty other men.
They all snore something terrible,
but at least it's out of the cold."
"They let you drink there?" I asked.
"No, but we all do," he said.
He looked at me and then said,
"You're still young. You should find
someone to love while you still can."
"I've got to go now," I said,
and handed him a five dollar bill.
"Thanks," he said.
"See you tomorrow," I said.
"I hope so," he said
and smiled.

MISDIRECTION

Misdirection is what magicians call it
when they make you watch their left hand go up
while their right hand snatches the ball out
from under the cup.

Misdirection is what street thieves use
when they bump your coffee so you almost drop it,
apologizing profusely
while taking your wallet from your back pocket.

And when it comes to slight-of-hand language
and the stealing of your brain,
politicians are masters
at the misdirection game.

Well... with a magician, people just applaud,
and with a pickpocket, you call the law,
and with a politician, you can organize the vote,
expose the fraud, do what's right,
or go out on strike,
...but what do you do about Life?
Isn't Life the biggest misdirection of all?
I mean, do you have any idea why we're here?
"Look at my left hand—here's marriage and a career!"
Any idea what it's all about?
"Hey don't worry, there's plenty of money in the account."
Any idea who you were before you were born?
"Hey come on over, there's a party in the dorm."
Any idea what it's like to die?
Any idea what's on the other side?
Any idea what love really is?
Any idea why we were born human
and not ravens or crows?

"Ah, you only live once, you know."
...Well maybe we don't.
Maybe we live over and over and over
and over and over again,
and maybe this thing called Life
is itself
just
one
big
misdirection.

BUT YOU CAN

They say that life gets better,
but it doesn't.
Life is just life, buddy,
and it doesn't give a shit about you.
Life doesn't get better,
but you can.

What is life?
You spin around the sun 60 or 70 times,
and then you die.
The revolutions don't vary,
only you do.

Are you everything you wanted to be?
I'm not.
But I'm still trying.

I know it's fashionable to say,
"Don't try, just do it,"
but you can't do it
without trying to do it first.

So try,
try to make it better,
try to be a better person.

Life doesn't get any better,
but you can.

NO OTHER CHOICE

I don't know about you,
but my job is to transform my life into art.
I think that's your job too—
to transform your life into art.
I think that's what we're here to do—
to transform our lives into art...
into music or poems or stories or pictures...
collages of color that build and cascade...
to turn our pain into rainbows,
because we have no other choice...
Nothing else cures the pain...
Nothing else cures the pain.
We are only here for such a short time.
You don't believe me because you are young,
but we are like butterflies that only live a week,
dipping our tongues into flowers
before we crumple to the ground...
and once life is gone, it's gone...
My job is to transform my life into art.
Your job is to transform your life into art.
Our job is to transform our lives into art.

ABOUT THE AUTHOR

For over fifty years, Robert Rahula has published dozens of books of prose and poetry in Spain and the United States. While he remains relatively undiscovered in the United States, he is revered in Spain as the founder of the *portilla* style of popular Spanish poetry: non-metered fluid verse that deals with love, loss, bisexuality, separateness, and growing older.

He was born in Spain to an American father and Spanish mother but grew up in Virginia on the farm of his paternal grandparents. He returned to Menorca, Spain, in the 1960s to pursue his writing career. These days he travels in Europe and Central and South America for several months a year giving readings and lectures. He spends the rest of his time writing and divides his time between Spain and the United States.

All of his English books are available, including his groundbreaking erotic novel *Messieurs*, his second English novel *Panamaniac*, his erotic murder mystery *Island of Misfits*, his surreal novel *Day Another Paradise In*, his acclaimed supernatural novel *One Last Fling*, his "sexistential" novel *Conversations in a Belgian Bar*, his "memoir" *A Modest Summation of Things*, as well as his Dan Landes Mystery novels: *Bathhouse Stories, All the Yage in Reno, Exigent Circumstances*, and *Uninvited Guest*.

Eight volumes of his English poetry are also available: *Trigger Points, Inside the Locked Heart, Camino, Migration, I Sing the Body Politic, Wonderland, From Whose Bourn, Expat Poems,* an anthology of his English poems and short stories *(Half-Life)*, and a collection of his most famous Spanish poems *(Poemas Españoles)*. Other poems, along with his blog on writing and his tour itinerary, appear on his Facebook page and on his website robertrahula.com.

www.ingramcontent.com/pod-product-compliance
Lightning Source LLC
Chambersburg PA
CBHW071215080526
44587CB00013BA/1389